MORE THAN BRICKS AND MORTAR

A History of the

Atlanta Athletic Club

MORE THAN BRICKS AND MORTAR

A History of the

Atlanta Athletic Club

By

Nancy Neill

WH Wolfe Associates
Historical Publications Division
P. O. Box 972
Roswell, Georgia 30077

Library of Congress
Cataloging in Publication
Card Number 87-51024

ISBN: 0-9613474-2-2

WH Wolfe Associates
Historical Publications Division
P. O. Box 972
Roswell, Georgia 30077

Table of Contents

Introduction

"As a teenager I lived across the street from the fourth tee. And in the mornings I would look out on that golf course. The sun used to come up over that grass, with all the dew on it. It sparkled like diamonds. Things like that used to make a big difference in my life."

— Eugene E. Brooks

*O*ne of the easy fallacies we fall prey to in twentieth-century U.S. culture is that business life is important and social life is not all that important. If a single lesson can be learned from the interviews that have gone into the preparation of this book, it is that social institutions can be infinitely important to the lives of individuals. As longtime member Eugene Brooks says, they can make a big difference.

Many months after I had begun interviewing the older members of the club for their recollections of the early days, and reading the old *Club Times,* I ran across a profile of "Colonel Bob" Jones, Bobby Jones' father. "He is part of the soul of East Lake," the writer said, "one of the personalities who kept us going as something more than just brick and stone and lake and green and fairway." It later occurred to me the theme of this history lay in those words. The Atlanta Athletic Club has been much more than bricks and mortar to a lot of people. It has been the center of many of life's rituals and pleasures. And because the friends remained the same, the facility the club happened to be housed in was secondary. That underlying strength is what has allowed this club to adapt and prosper in the face of economic and social pressures for almost a century.

The crises the club has undergone — fires, the Great Depression, relocation — give this history its depth. The high moments of celebration include the club's nearly simultaneous 1926 openings of a grand new town facility on Carnegie Way and a stately country club at East Lake (to replace a clubhouse destroyed in a fire); that glory of glories, the 1930 winning of the Grand Slam of golf by member Bobby Jones; and that rite of passage that acknowledges a club's standing in the golfing world, the first-time hosting of the U.S. Open in 1976.

Atlanta's newspapers provided many of the details of these events. Others came from Franklin Garrett's *Atlanta and Environs,* an indispensable repository of details about Atlanta's history. Herbert Warren Wind's *The Story of American Golf* provided a national and international perspective on golf and other sports. And I am much indebted to Charles Elliott, a club member who compiled a history of the club in the early 1970s. To bring the events in the club's history to life, many of its members spent long afternoons describing to me memories that stretch back to the early part of this century, when, as the first chapter shows, Atlanta was more country town than big city.

In getting the book into print, I am again indebted to Franklin Garrett, who was kind enough to review the manuscript for historical accuracy. And to Jim Petzing, Jodi Wolfe, Carol Stewart, and Delaris Dukes ("DD") Cavanagh — members of the staff at the club — who provided assistance and information along the way.

Chapter One

Swell Buckboards, High Spirits

$\mathcal{A}$tlanta in the late 1890s was still as much country town as city. Men still gathered of a summer afternoon on the street corners at Five Points — at Jacobs' corner where Marietta Street intersected Peachtree Street and near Tyner's drugstore at Marietta and Broad. Lawyers, dry goods clerks, bank clerks, and stenographers whiled away the time, tucking their thumbs into the armholes of their vests and swapping stories as their smoke billowed on the summer's breeze.

"Atlanta was a pleasant, easy-going place in which to live," writes Atlanta historian Franklin M. Garrett in *Atlanta and Environs*. "Gentlemen were gentlemen and ladies were ladies in every sense of the word. Men worked hard, but without nervous tension, and nearly everyone took the time and effort to be gracious. . . . The famous Atlanta spirit was in flower too, and any worthy cause or progressive idea drew immediate support and financial backing from civic leaders."

Rising Interest in Sports

It was in this atmosphere of small-town friendliness and big-city promise that a young lawyer, Burton Smith, conceived of a social institution that would become an important part of the fabric of Atlanta in the next century — the Atlanta Athletic Club.

Smith, the son of a professor at the University of North Carolina, had taken a bachelor's degree in philosophy at the University of Georgia and moved to Atlanta to enter the law practice of his brother Hoke (who served in the cabinet of President Grover Cleveland and was later to become governor of Georgia). By 1898, Smith, 32, had "read law," been admitted to the bar, and practiced for a number of years. His "decidedly swell buckboard" was often seen on Atlanta's streets, along with the handsome landaus, dos-a-dos carriages, broughams, stanhopes, and Tuxedo wagons of the day, according to the June 14, 1891, *Atlanta Constitution*.

Portrait of Burton Smith, whose idea it was to form a club where he and his friends could enjoy indoor as well as outdoor athletics.

It was in the summer of 1898, thinking of the fall and winter months ahead, that he began to toy with the idea of starting a club where he and his friends and business associates could enjoy indoor as well as outdoor athletics.

Atlanta was not without its social clubs at the time. In fact, two had been founded within the previous fifteen years. The Capital City Club, Atlanta's first social club, had been started in 1883 by four young men who had tired of the overflow evening crowds in the lobby and billiard rooms of the Kimball House hotel. The second, the Gentlemen's Driving Association (later renamed the Piedmont Driving Club), was started in 1887 by a group of young horse lovers who wanted a pleasant place to exercise and show off their mounts.

Smith may have had the successes of these clubs in mind when he began to imagine an athletic club. More likely, a natural athlete himself, he was stimulated by the rising tide of interest in athletics throughout the United States, particularly amateur athletics.

Many of the sports attracting interest were new

to the United States, if not to the world. Football was the runaway favorite. It had been introduced at Princeton and Rutgers in 1869, and by the time the University of Georgia and Auburn teams tangled for the first time, in Piedmont Park in February 1892, the city hailed football as a great new sport. Georgia Tech and the University of Georgia began their classic confrontations the next year.

Tennis had also gained a lively following, particularly after the national championships were started at the Newport Casino in 1881. And basketball had been invented within the decade — by Dr. James Naismith at Springfield College in 1891 when, according to legend, he asked the janitor to nail up a pair of peach baskets in the gym. Track and field sports had also caught the public's fancy with the first modern Olympic Games in 1896. All these new sports presented an irresistible challenge to the young man who prided himself on his athletic prowess.

Birth of AAC

The time was right for Burton Smith's idea, and it "took" immediately. Within a month he had presented it to his friends and business associates, incorporated, and attracted 64 other members. The event was detailed in an article in the *Atlanta Journal Magazine* on January 4, 1914, some 16 years later:

It was in August, 1898, that Burton Smith conceived the idea of organizing an athletic club. Mr. Smith was then and is now of superb athletic build and inclinations, and it is peculiarly appropriate that he should be the one to found the institution. He acted upon his idea at once. He spoke to Arnold Broyles, and thus it fell out that the south's finest athletic organization sprang from the two men who would of all others be selected as her representative specimens of physical manhood. These two conferred with Ulric Atkinson, Henry Thornton, W. B. Roberts, Reuben Hayden, George Adair [Jr.] and one or two others about it [including Barnwell W. Dunlap and Colonel W. L. Peel]. These were all in sympathy with the idea. They met in Mr. Smith's law office on Broad street and formally organized the club on August 15, 1898.

The charter, which was granted on September 6, was signed by all 65 men. Some were lawyers and graduates of the University of Georgia, like Burton Smith, Henry Porter, and Arnold Broyles. Some were realtors, like George W. Adair, Jr. Most were young men, in their early- to mid-twenties,

with Smith and Broyles (in their thirties) capping off the age range.

The purpose of the club was stated briefly in the charter: "The object of this corporation is not pecuniary gain, but the formation of a social club, the special purpose of which is preparing and maintaining a gymnasium and enjoying physical exercise." The initiation fee was set at $25 and annual dues were $24.

Not surprisingly, it was Burton Smith who became the first president of the club, with R. C. Hayden as vice president, W. B. Roberts as secretary, and B. S. Dunlap as treasurer. Directors the first year were A. M. Hoke, James R. McKeldin, Henry Thornton, Henry Porter, W. L. Peel, W. A. Matthews, M. M. Jackson, and Ulric Atkinson.

The first order of business was to establish a facility. The members first looked around for a third floor hall or a loft in an existing building, but as so often would happen in the club's future, something better was in store. The *Atlanta Journal Magazine* of January 4, 1914, describes what the club's new facilities turned out to be: "Joel Hurt (one of the club's charter members) built a clubhouse on Edgewood Avenue, just below the Equitable building. This building . . . was leased then for a period of five years. The club had no money, but the members went ahead, confident of success. About $1,600 worth of apparatus was installed in the gymnasium which, with a miniature swimming pool and a tennis court, a checker board and a set of chess men, constituted the entire outfit of the Atlanta Athletic Club in the beginning of 1899." Apart from the gymnasium, which was considered well-equipped for the times, the club's quarters were spartan when they were officially opened on April 15, 1899. They included administrative offices, a lounge, locker rooms, and showers — no telephone and no dining facilities.

Early Success

The new Athletic Club, located so near Five Points, the heart of the business district, rode the crest of strong growth in Atlanta. The population of the city had risen at a rate of about 2,000 people a year since 1870 and the pace was quickening as the century-mark neared. By 1900, not much more than a year after the club was started, the population had reached almost 90,000.

The growth of the city brought new businesses and a constant flow of new members for the club's early years. The predecessor to the Trust Company Bank of Georgia, The Commercial Travelers' Savings Bank, and the predecessor to the Life Insurance Company of Georgia, then The Industrial Aid Association, were born in 1891; the Atlanta

Coca-Cola Bottling Company was formed to make Atlanta's new beverage available not only at soda fountains, but in bottles; the Atlanta Steel Hoop Company, later the Atlantic Steel Company, was started in 1901 so the South could manufacture its own bands for cotton bales and its own hoops for barrels; and in the same year AAC member Henry Atkinson acquired control of the Georgia Electric Light Company of Atlanta, which would later become the Georgia Power Company.

Another indication of the city's growth was the trade show of 1895, called the Cotton States and International Exposition. The show, held in Piedmont Park, attracted 6,000 exhibits and some 800,000 visitors in 199 days. On a single day 55,000 visitors came, a number more than two-thirds the size of the population of the city at the time. Many who came to Atlanta for the show decided to stay. One of those was Ivan E. Allen, who was to become both an AAC member and a community leader in Atlanta. The city, his son later observed in *The Atlanta Spirit*, "was fast outstripping other Southern cities which had missed the bus or been too proud to make terms with changing conditions."

The era of afternoon gatherings at the corners near Five Points and of stylish horse-drawn rigs would soon vanish, swept away by the growing commerce of the city and by the appearance, in 1901, of the first "horseless carriage" on Atlanta's streets.

In this environment, the Athletic Club was an immediate success. By 1901 membership had swelled to 700 (500 residents of Atlanta and 200 non-residents), and the club was fast becoming the tennis center of Atlanta. Two courts had been constructed on the vacant lot next to the Edgewood building. "It was on these courts that the club began to develop some of its younger players — such athletes as Nat Thornton, C. Y. Smith, E. V. Carter, Jr., Frank Owens and B. M. Grant," writes club historian Charles Elliott in his 1973 account of the club's history. Other members had formed a baseball team and in 1900, looking like streetcar motormen in the baseball dress of the day — stiff caps and beards — , laid claim to the city championship.

Before the Edgewood lease had expired, Burton Smith found himself negotiating for a new facility. The officers decided to build on a vacant lot on Auburn Avenue and commissioned architects Bleckley and Tyler to design the building. After four years in its original home at 56 Edgewood Avenue, the Atlanta Athletic Club moved on November 27, 1902, to 37 Auburn Avenue, one street away and still a stone's throw from Five Points. There it would prosper for almost a quarter of a century, nourished by the high spirits of a country town bent on becoming a city.

3

Chapter Two

Bean's Boys

*I*t was just a plain old red-brick, three-story building," remembers Charles Ponder, who joined the club in 1917. "Had a swimming pool on the lower floor, and on the main floor a couple of reading rooms and a gym where people worked out. The offices were on the second floor, and the third floor was where they had the pool room, with card tables in it, and the lunchroom. They didn't have a real fancy restaurant. It was just a small building, adequate for our needs."

By the standards of its time, however, the Auburn Avenue club was more than adequate. Instead of two, there were now four tennis courts. The new swimming pool was spacious. And there were new sports facilities: basketball and handball courts, an indoor track, pool tables, and a bowling alley. The locker room and showers were also substantially larger.

These enlarged facilities soon paid off. During the quarter-century the Athletic Club remained on Auburn Avenue, it produced Southern champions in basketball, tennis, track, and swimming, and city and state champions in baseball. Membership also rose steadily, as the club continued to benefit from the city's growth.

Of all the teams, it is the basketball team that generated the most colorful tales about the club's early days on Auburn.

Basketball on Auburn

In 1903 the club's basketball team played its first game; it was against Yale, and the club lost. The next year the players hit the boards in earnest, and with the help of Dr. Theodore "Ted" Toeppel, who was hired as physical director in 1905, they soon became a competitive team.

In 1908 the club hired John W. Heisman, then Georgia Tech's first football coach [later founder of the Heisman Football Trophy] as physical director and basketball coach, at a salary of $75 a month. Heisman reportedly knew nothing about

Joe Bean, a tough, wiry Irishman, made basketball a highlight of club life.

basketball when he started. But he had soon put together a team that could hold its own in the raucous hoop and hardwood environment of the day — taking on other athletic clubs, such as the Birmingham and Macon athletic clubs; colleges, such as the University of Georgia, Georgia Tech, Auburn, and Alabama; and anyone else who would venture onto the courts.

The gyms were sometimes makeshift affairs. "One year at Georgia we played in a building upstairs that was a former skating rink made into a gym," remembers Ralph Williams, who played on AAC's team. "At the University of Kentucky we played in a band box. They had chicken wire in front of the seats and along the side . . . Auburn had a court like that, too."

Nat Thornton, younger brother of founding

member Henry Thornton, described the brand of basketball they played in a November 1968 *Club Times*:

> We had a rugged and rough basketball team. We could whip any college five that came along. One of the fellows I remember in our bunch was Al Doolittle. There was another player whose name I can't recall, but he was a professional wrestler. He used to knock opposing players right and left. The referee didn't call many fouls in those days — you had to hit a man with your fist, or almost kill him, before they called a foul on you.
>
> I recollect one game we played with Birmingham Athletic Club. The Birmingham boys were our most bitter rivals. That affair looked more like a free-for-all fight than a basketball game. The main object was to lay 'em out and we did a good job of that. We shook 'em up so bad that a little college team — Vanderbilt — beat them the next night.

This rough-hewed AAC team, a forerunner to today's hockey teams, won its first Southern championship in 1909.

In 1911, the club hired a physical director and coach who would lead the team to its second Southern championship in 1913 — Joe Bean. (He was also athletic director and coach at Marist College at the time.) Bean was the small, wiry type of athlete Heisman would have rejected from his Georgia Tech football team without a second glance. Weighing in at all of 113 pounds, Bean had managed to make the baseball minor leagues at 20; earned his way into the New York Giants' club in 1902; and, later, played for the New Jersey baseball club. A likeable man, he quickly captured the respect and affection of the Athletic Club basketball team. "He was a tough Irishman and would get pretty profane during a game," says Williams. "But he was a good-hearted person — do anything for you."

Bean's Saturday night basketball games were a highlight of the club's social activities. Members and their wives or dates crowded into the limited spectator area and chanted their pleasure or displeasure at the goings-on. The game was played by different rules then. After every basket, both teams barrelled back to center court for a jumpoff (the club's team in dark blue uniforms with "AAC" emblazoned on the front). A foul in favor of AAC brought a roar of victory from the crowd because, under the rules of the day, the best shooter on the team took all the foul shots. The crowd's enthusiasm spilled over into the dances that always followed the games.

Bean reeled off the names of many players of the time in an interview with Elliott: ". . . Al Doonan, Luther Hudson, Nat Thornton, Tommy Atkinson, Leo Spencer, Dick Jamison, Joe Colquitt, Fred Hoyt, Halsey McGovern, Tillou Forbes, Jim Harrison, Edwin Haas, and a boy named Post who was an exceptionally fine player." One of these players, Dick Jamison, was sports editor for *The Atlanta Constitution* at the time and his coverage was unapologetically biased. Says Charles Ponder, "I'll never forget one article he wrote for the Sunday paper. The Athletic Club had beaten the Birmingham Club the night before and Mr. Jamison was the shooter. He wrote, 'As usual, Dick Jamison made 19 straight foul shots.'"

The next generation of AAC players, according to Bean, included many of the outstanding players in the South, such as "Ed and Frank Carter, Walter Dubard, Lamax Pie Weaver, Willingham Smith, John Groves, Johnny Westmoreland, Scrappy O'Sullivan, and many more of high playing ability." To that list Ralph Williams, a player on the team in the mid-1920s, adds a few: "Rufus Bass, Joe Singleton, Pat Stevens, Monk Johnson, Bill Morrow, Alfred Scott, Steve Hartney, Tom Bryan, Ronnie Morrison, and Henry Cop." He characterizes the play in this way: "The games themselves were for he-men and often even the fittest didn't survive. How the fans liked it!"

The AAC team was either winner or runner-up in the Southern Basketball Tournament every year from 1912 to 1926, when competition as a club team ended, for the time being. In a December 1925 article in *The City Builder*, Atlanta's Chamber of Commerce publication, sportswriter Morgan Blake proclaimed: "Atlanta — the unquestioned basketball center of Dixie, with its annual colorful southern tournaments with twenty or more colleges represented. Atlanta — home of the Beanboys, famous Atlanta Athletic club basketball team, nearly always the best basketball team in the south, and always a very close contender."

Tennis, AAC's Top Sport

While basketball seemed to attract a great deal of the spotlight, tennis was the top sport at the club in the early decades of the century, led by those young players who had begun to shape their skills on the courts at Edgewood — Nat Thornton, Carleton Y. Smith, and B. M. Grant, all of whom would win the Southern Singles Championship one or more times. Smith would claim the title five times between 1912 and 1921.

Thornton recalls those days in the November 1968 *Club Times* article:

> They took me in before I was old enough to be a regular member . . . because I won a

tournament. I beat Sam Williams easy. Sam, an insurance man, hired me to work for him, because he wanted me to go all over the country and play tennis. I was not required to pay dues because I was playing as a member of the club. I won forty or fifty cups playing tennis all over the south. Some I remember were the Gulf States in New Orleans, three times, the Old Dominion in Richmond, twice — and I never did go back for a third try — the Tennessee State and South Atlantic State three times — that was before they expanded it into the Southern, and I won that three times, too.

Bryan Grant and I won the doubles nearly every year. Bryan was Bitsey's father. Bitsey never would learn to hit the ball. All he'd do was pat it back, but he was the best in the world at that.

They were victorious times, as Morgan Blake attests in the continuation of his 1925 paean to the Athletic Club: "Atlanta — home of tennis champions; of Carleton Smith, greatest of all southern tennis players and winner of so many southern championships that it became monotonous. Atlanta — home of Jeff Hunt, present southern champion, and of Frank Owens and Nat Thornton."

By 1929 the sport had become so popular in Atlanta that nearly every golf club in the city had added tennis courts, and facilities had been built at the Piedmont Driving Club and the Atlanta Tennis Club. The city also offered a choice of fifty-nine public courts, most of them at Grant Park and Piedmont Park, and most of them, like the private club courts, of sand clay construction.

But it was indisputably the Athletic Club that led the field. Thornton, Smith, Grant, and other AAC players — Ed Carter; Frank ("Hop") Owens (Southern Tennis Singles Champion in 1923); E. S. Mansfield; J. D. Hunt; Jack Caldwell; Jack Mooney; Jake Orr; Carl Ramspeck; and the son of B. M. Grant, Bryan, Jr. ("Bitsy" or "Bitsey"). Bitsy Grant alone won ten Southern Tennis Singles and four National Clay Court Singles championships. These outstanding AAC players would maintain tennis supremacy in the South for more than

Tennis was the top sport at the club in the early days. 1. ——, 2. Burt Adams, 3. Cowan Rogers, 4. Frank Reynolds, 5. Charlie Rogers, 6. Stirling Blackshear, 7. ——, 8. Geo. Adair, 9. H.M. Ashe, 10. Lew Scott, 11. R.G. Hunt (Cal), 12. Sawyer, 13. R.D. Little (Cin. Ohio), 14. Tich Tichenor, 15. Arthur Howell, 16. Carl Ramspeck, 17. Lee, 18. Bland Logan (N.O.), 19. Carleton Smith, 20. Bryan Grant, 21. Auderby Post (N.O.), 22. Nat Thornton, 23. Miss Logan (N.J.), 24. Cathleen Brown, 25. ——, 26. ——, 27. Prof. Mooney (Tenn.), 28. Freeman, 29. Coke Davis, 30. — ——, 31. Foster Fitzsimmons, 32. Howard Mathews, 33. Ed Taylor (Macon), 34. Will Gunn, 35. F.G. Byrd, 36. Bill Kemp, 37. ——, 38. ——, 39. Bill Patterson, 40. ——, Dot Berrian, 42. ——, Fielding Smith, 43. ——, 44. ——, 45. ——.

three decades, from 1907 to 1940, taking 21 of 34 Southern Tennis Singles championships.

In addition to participating successfully in serious competitive play, AAC members kept up their share of tomfoolery. "Somebody was always playing a trick or pulling a shenanigan," remembered Fred Patterson (who joined AAC in 1903) in a February 1970 *Club Times* article. "Jake Orr, for instance, once bet he could take on and beat anything in his crowd at tennis, even with a brick tied to one foot. He got a bet out of that in a hurry, so he tied the brick to his foot, but with a string about forty feet long that didn't hinder him from moving around the court."

The baseball team won the title of Amateur Champions of Georgia. L-R, top row: Geo. Spence, Burt Adams, Will Glenn, Frank Reynolds, Carleton Smith, John Gore. 2nd row: Tich Tichenor, Arthur Howell, Geo. Adair, Bill Patterson. 1st row: Alvin Haynes, F.G. Byrd, Nat Thornton.

While tennis was the most popular sport when the Auburn Avenue club opened, other sports had attracted a following. The indoor baseball team won the city title in 1904, and with the arrival of Toeppel as physical director in 1908, the outdoor baseball team went on to win the title of Amateur Champions of Georgia. Both indoor and outdoor track were popular. The first member of the club to show an interest in track was Walter Scott, who won the annual road races in Birmingham three times. When the Southern Championship Road Race was held at Grant Field in 1911, the AAC's team was the winning team. The swimming team, which included Gilbert Fraser, Homer Thompson, and Mariana Goldsmith (later Knox), first competed in 1915 and became Southern champions in 1917.

Those who didn't participate in team sports often found time to work out at the club during lunch or after work, when Bean regularly conducted classes. "The physical fitness classes were well attended by such prominent members as Paul Fleming, ex-Governor John M. Slaton, Dr. Angier Fred Gould, Lynn Werner, Fred Stockes, Frank Eastman, Uncle Jack Stewart, Henry and Charlie Floyd, Tom Higdon, and others whose names I can't recall at this time," Bean said. "This was a most congenial group. They generally wound up with a swim in the pool, which was not heated and at times during the winter months was extremely cold. The lunch that followed was a dish of turnip greens, side meat, cornbread, and buttermilk, eaten sitting astride a bench in the locker room."

In all the club's athletic activities the continued, enthusiastic presence of Joe Bean encouraged members to participate and excel. It was the beginning of an era of stability and increasing participation that would last through three generations of members.

AAC tennis players were supreme in the South for more than three decades. L — R: Bitsy Grant, Tom Bird, Eugene Branch, Joe Becknell (pro) and Lang Shippey.

A New Sport

While these various teams were winning recognition for the Athletic Club, changes in the leadership of the club were occurring that would introduce a new sport — and even greater recognition.

With the Athletic Club now an accepted Atlanta institution, Burton Smith resigned the presidency shortly after the move to Auburn. His vice president, Arnold Broyles, took the reins, providing continuity in leadership for the early years. Like Smith, Broyles was a lawyer and a graduate of the University of Georgia. A native Georgian, born in Rome, he was also active in politics. He was Mayor Pro Tem in 1894, was elected a state representative for the term 1894-1895, and became clerk of the Superior Court of Fulton County in 1900, a position he held for many years.

It was his successor, George Adair, Jr., president from 1905 to 1911, who would change the athletic direction of the club. During the years of Broyles' presidency, Adair began lobbying for the Atlanta Athletic Club to be the first club in the city to provide a permanent course for the game of golf, which had only recently gained a following in the United States. It was a dream soon to be realized — one that would stamp the identity of the club firmly in the minds of Atlantans, bring the club to the attention of the entire world, and ensure its success more than any previous sport.

A Growing City

Changes were occurring in Atlanta that would

also contribute to the club's success and shape its future. The city continued to grow: two newspapers were born in the first decade of the new century, *The Atlanta News* and *The Atlanta Georgian*; in 1905 a new Terminal Station opened to the strains of "Down in Dixie"; and in 1906 Atlantans watched a new skyscraper rise, the 17-story Candler building, commissioned by Asa G. Candler. "High as the Candler building" was added to the local lexicon.

The automobile also began to "shorten" the distance between downtown Atlanta and outlying areas. Atlanta's business district still ended a half-mile north of Five Points, where Davison's department store and the Peachtree Plaza hotel now stand. There, a solemnity of church spires and grand residences, set back from the traffic on tree-shaded lawns, indicated the end of commerce and the beginning of community life. But by 1904 it was routine to see automobiles chugging along in front of these homes at a heady 8 miles per hour (the speed limit inside the city's "fire limits"). Even at that measured pace, the vehicles occasionally collided with surreys and caused indignant reprimands.

One somber change was the failure of an Atlanta bank, the Neal Bank (E. H. Thornton, president), touched off by the failure of a bank in New York. Though it foreshadowed the failures that would attend the stock market crash in 1929, the Atlanta of the first decade shrugged it off as an anomaly.

Another event gave immediate and unexpected impetus to the growth of Atlanta's clubs — prohibition. In 1907 the city outlawed public sale

9

of liquor, ending, in the words of Franklin Garrett, the era of "the swinging door, brass rail, free lunch, and whiskey by the drink." In all, 132 whiskey and beer houses were closed; barber shops, office supply stores, lunch rooms, meat markets, and furniture stores replaced them.

So did private clubs. As Garrett explains in his history, "There were some loopholes in the prohibition law of 1907. Clubs were permitted to serve drinks to their members. This was done on the assumption that a club, especially in Atlanta, where clubs dominate social life, was a man's home — his second home at least. So the bars in Atlanta's legitimate clubs were kept open as usual."

The new era for the Athletic Club was begun. An era of good times, competitive team sports, and a dream of golf leadership soon to be realized. There was plenty to celebrate, and holiday parties were as high-spirited as Joe Bean's basketball games. Bean recalls the traditional Christmas Day festivities: "Eggnog was served in large tubs on the gym floor — and what eggnog that was! This party wound up in the pool, with people swimming on hundred pound cakes of ice. Oh boy, what a day!"

Chapter Three

A Country Club

"Most of our successful tournament players have come up as caddy boys, like Sarazen, Hogan, and Nelson or, like myself, as sons of members of golf clubs, turned out to pasture with a cleek or two and a few balls."

— Bobby Jones

On a summer night in 1908 a 6-year-old, somewhat frail boy named Bobby Jones climbed into his bed on the sleeping porch of a summer home at East Lake Country Club. He drifted off into the pleasantest of dreams, holding in his arms the tiny, three-inch-high silver trophy he had won in a golf tournament that day.

It was only a neighborhood tournament, a children's pastime arranged by the Jones' friend, Mrs. Frank Meador, for Bobby, her son Frank, the slightly older Perry Adair, and little redheaded Alexa Stirling. Or so it must have seemed. In fact, as the club would realize in retrospect, it was a tournament of child prodigies. In the next two decades Perry would win the Southern Amateur Championship twice, Alexa would capture three national championships, and Bobby would go all the way to the top to win golfing's greatest prize — the Grand Slam.

Golf Comes to Atlanta

That night was still eight years in the future when Perry's father George Adair began to lobby the membership of the Athletic Club to build a golf course.

Golf had made its way over from Europe in the late 1700s. Savannah, Georgia, had a golf club in 1800 (which was disbanded at the start of the War of 1812). But it was not until the latter part of the century, when the Athletic Club was founded, that golf became popular in this country. The first permanent golf club was started in 1888 in Ardsley, New York (Yonkers), a 6-hole course on 30 acres of pasture. And within a decade the sport had spread all over the United States. By 1900 some 250,000 people were playing golf and at least one course had been built in every state.

The 1890s had seen two efforts to introduce golf to Atlanta. The Piedmont Driving Club had laid out a 7-hole course in 1896, but interest had not been high enough to maintain the course. And in 1898, 27 men and women had opened an unsodded course called "Brookstone" at Kirkwood, about 15 minutes by streetcar from the city. (The five ladies played in Gibson girl outfits of sailor hats, heavy linen skirts, high-button shoes, and blouses with muttonchop sleeves.) This effort, too, was short-lived. But the interest in golf lingered, and under Adair's advocacy the Athletic Club began to believe it was the institution that could successfully introduce this sport to Atlanta and the Southeast.

In 1904 the club decided to buy property for a country club that would offer golf along with the established club sports. Since the streetcar line had been extended toward an area called East Lake, that seemed a likely spot. Charles Elliott describes what East Lake was like at the time: "East Lake itself, a sparkling stretch of water surrounded by forest land, was the site of an amusement park run by Tom Poole. It was privately owned and its chief attractions were a swimming beach, picnic tables, hotdog-popcorn-and-peanut stands, and a penny arcade where for the sum of one cent, people could peep at such scenes as Pike's Peak, the 1889 World's Fair in faraway Paris, the Eiffel Tower (which opened that same year), and bathing beauties in revealing bloomers. There was also a real steamboat that huffed and puffed up and down the narrow confines of the lake to give sightseers a thrilling ride."

AAC member Harry M. Atkinson was the owner of the property. Born in Massachusetts and educated at Harvard, he had played golf many times. When Adair approached him about the property, he was immediately enthusiastic. "You may have it at your own figure," he replied, according to a 1939 article in *The Atlanta Constitution* by sports columnist and AAC member O. B. Keeler. Adair left not only with a favorable purchase price but with a contribution to the clubhouse building fund. He then arranged for Asa G. Candler to buy the rest of the grounds the club needed and to exchange the land for a tract of similar size nearby.

East Lake Country Club

A country club was a first for Atlanta. The Capital City Club had only its downtown facility at the time, and the Piedmont Driving Club, though some distance from downtown, emphasized its social functions more than its outdoor activities.

Four AAC golfers pause for a photo in their "plus fours."

Mrs. Thomas B. Paine tries her hand at the new game of golf.

The land purchase was greeted with hyperbole in *The Atlanta Journal* on July 7, 1904:

Atlanta at last is to have a real, live, up-to-date country club, grounded on the most select pattern and style, with every modern convenience for athletic and social enjoyment for the 500 members desired.

For this movement the beautiful grounds surrounding East Lake, at least 160 acres of typical country club surroundings, have been secured and the spot chosen is an almost ideally perfect one for the undertaking. The purchase price will amount to $25,000 and $25,000 additional outlay will be placed on the erection of a suitable club house. . . .

The athletic life of the club will embrace every form of outdoor sport. An 18-hole golf course will be laid out and the club will enter the United States Golf Association, holding not only southern tournaments, but drawing to Atlanta the star performers of the entire country in mid-winter tourneys.

But golf will not embrace the entire category: The finest bowling greens in the south will be erected; tennis courts will be built; gun club recreation for trap and pigeon lovers, and in fact a complete chain of all sports known to modern civilization are included. Then the lake offers attractions for boating and rowing and a modern boat house is included in the prospective plans.

Atlantans were primed and waiting for this new kind of social institution.

Development of the property, actually 187 acres including the 30-acre lake, proceeded more gradually than the newspaper implied it would. When Adair assumed the presidency of the club in 1905, the board voted to commission the building of a 7-hole golf course, to be designed by course architect Tom Bendelow. It took almost two years, according to Charles Elliott, "to hack the space for fairways, tees, and greens out of the forested hillsides, to grade and shape, and grow a stand of grass on the reluctant red soil. What heavy machinery there was consisted of scoops, graders and mowers, all powered by mules. Most of the work to bring the new golf course into existence was done by hand, with axe and saw, and pick and shovel."

The course was soon enlarged to 9 holes and then to 18. "They must have been amazed at what they found they had bought out there," says Arch Martin. "The land was a rectangular bowl that sloped from all directions down toward the middle where the lake was. The slope was gentle. The four corners of the rectangle were just about the high points on the golf course. The first time I saw that course was in 1912, when my father joined out there. You could see all over the place from just about any spot on the thing. They had one nine on one side of the lake and a nine on the other. I don't know if they knew all that when they bought it, but it certainly turned out to be a beautiful thing."

Shortly after the course was completed, the club held its first Southern championship, won by Lawrence Eustace of New Orleans. The club also gained prestige by attracting as its pro Alex Smith, winner of both the Western Open and the U.S. Open in 1906. A native of Carnoustie, Scotland, he was one of five brothers who came to the United States in the 1890s and helped spread the popularity of golf. He also knew how to make golf clubs, setting a tradition for the pros who followed him at East Lake.

As Adair was convinced it would, the Athletic Club proved to be a natural sponsor for the new game of golf. The early years at East Lake were years of constant construction, to keep up with the growing popularity of golf among the members and to keep up with the other activities of country club life.

First, the Athletic Club decided to expand East Lake's non-golfing facilities. The board had several tennis courts constructed, had the lake area developed for swimming and boating, and commissioned architect Edward E. Daugherty to design an enlarged bath- and boat house. With about 1,000 Atlantans now owning automobiles, the club also decided to construct a half-mile automobile driveway at the entrance to the club's property.

Before long, the Club decided a clubhouse was needed at East Lake to keep up with the social activities demanded by members, and it commissioned Harry Leslie Walker to design a house with lockers, showers, and other accommodations. Anticipation ran high as the construction proceeded, and it was apparent that opening day would be a major event in the city's social calendar.

A Country Clubhouse

On July 4, 1908, East Lake Country Club came into its own. Both the new $45,000 clubhouse and the expanded course were opened that day, and it was the most popular spot in the city for the holiday. Members and guests arrived along a broad driveway lined with trees. Before them, set on a rise in the midst of the club's grounds, stood the new country clubhouse. And around the clubhouse was the new course, ringed with thick woods lush from recent rains.

The afternoon started with a 4:00 reception, hosted by President George Adair and his wife and attended by club members, their wives, sweethearts, and sisters. The "gentlemen's reception committee" included Thomas B. Paine, Lowry Arnold, Clarence Haverty, Arthur Clarke, Lewis

Gregg, J. W. Goldsmith, Walter Colquitt, W. H. Glenn, Forrest Adair, R. P. Jones, and Winship Nunnally. Serving afternoon tea were Mrs. Preston Arkwright, Mrs. John A. Fitten, Mrs. Lowry Arnold, Mrs. T. B. Paine, Mrs. J. H. Porter, Mrs. W. H. Glenn, Miss Florence Jackson, Miss Roline Clarke, Miss Edna McCandless, Miss Caroline DuBose, and Miss Elizabeth Adair.

After the reception members strolled the verandas of the new facility or wandered back to the lake, where a painted canoe parade was in progress, with 20 canoes competing for a prize. The society section of the July 5, 1908, *Atlanta Constitution* gave this description of the new facility:

> The club house consists of three stories, with buffet, bowling alleys, locker rooms and baths downstairs, bed rooms upstairs, and the main floor devoted to parlors and waiting rooms opening upon the large main reception hall, which will be used also as the ball room.
> The main reception room is one of splendid size and proportion. It extends the length of the building, the parlors opening out at each side, and its height is not limited by the upper story, since all the bed rooms are built around a balcony, which overlooks the reception hall. . .
> An orchestra last night played for dancing, and downstairs dinner was served in the attractive cafe. . . . The bright gathering of gayly gowned women who were present would have made less artistic surroundings attractive, and although there are nine hundred men belonging to the club, there was no overwhelming number of stags in evidence, but the goodly company of young ladies and married women, who were the guests of the club, offered emphatic suggestion of the enthusiastic pleasure Atlanta women feel in the hospitality which the Athletic Club has offered ladies since the beginning of its country club life and will continue to offer.
> There was no elaborate dressing among the women who were present, that simplicity which should be characteristic of country club attire being observed on this occasion as on all others at East Lake.
> Linen suits in white and colors and flowered or lingerie hats were universal, and afforded striking proof that the freshness and smartness of such a toilette has a charm of its own quite as satisfying as the elaborateness of laces and plumes.
> It is just this element of simplicity and that other element of yesterday's enjoyment — an informality which is at once bright and restful — that promises the lasting success of the country club.

It was a day of great celebration for club members, visible evidence of the entrepreneurism that had led the club to sponsor both a new sport for Atlanta and a new kind of social institution.

For all the celebration of the new course, golf

13

Fourteenth tee on the original course at East Lake. The site of the present second green is the hill in the background. The Mule House sat to the right of the tree and tower. Man on tee, Robert P. Jones. Extreme right, W.J Holloman. Boy seated on bench, Bobby Jones.

was still a minor interest compared to tennis. And on the day of the new club's opening, many members were talking about the Southern Tennis Meet, which would be held there the following week. For the first time, AAC would have sleeping quarters to offer its out-of-town guests.

A Boy Knocks Their Socks Off

But the core of golfers was growing. To begin with, there were F. G. Byrd, W. P. Hill, and Lowry Arnold, all experienced golfers. And under their wing, a number of good golfers developed at East Lake: George Adair, Reynolds Tichenor, S. C. Williams, Charles P. King, Dowdell Brown, W. K. Stone, Hamilton Block, W. H. Glenn, Frank Meador, Fulton Colville, Colonel and Mrs. (Clara) Robert P. Jones, Richard Hickey, Tom Prescott, the Thomas Paines, Edgar Ballenger, Clarence Knowles, Carleton Smith, Eston Mansfield, and Fred Patterson, among others. Atlantans were soon predictably strong contenders for the Southern championship.

And, of course, there was that younger set. This was the same year 6-year-old Bobby Jones played the 6-hole tournament with his friends, all of them using sawed-off clubs. And it was this younger set that would bring the new country club to the attention of the world.

Bobby had suffered a bad year when he was 5, contracting several childhood diseases one after another, including whooping cough and measles. To get him into the country air, his parents, who then lived in an apartment on West Peachtree, moved for the summer to a big boarding house near the country club that was owned by Mrs. Meador and that Jones later described as being "about a mashie pitch from what then was the second fairway." Bobby and Frank, who was two years older, were taken in hand by other boarders who were learning the game of golf at East Lake's unfinished course, as were Bobby's parents. One of them, Fulton Colville, sawed off a cleek (a No. 1 iron) and gave it to Bobby.

Since Frank and Bobby were too young to play on the course, they made their own course. The red clay road in front of the Meadors' house was their fairway. One hole was in front of the house and one was in a drainage ditch. "It is general opinion," Bobby Jones later said, "that I never made a hole-in-one until 1927. As a matter of fact, I made that ditch hole many times in one before I was 6 years old."

Golf might have remained only a passing interest for young Bobby, who was more enthusiastic about tennis and swimming, but the next year his family moved into a cottage on the grounds of the club itself — the old "Mule House" (so-called because it had housed livestock before it was renovated into a summer house). It was in this house that Bobby slept so pleasantly after winning his first tournament.

That year Bobby's mother and father would let him follow them around the course with his clubs, which included a brassie cut down from one of his mother's clubs, a mashie discarded by his dad, and the cleek, which he used for most of his shots. Knowing that he was expected not to delay their game, he developed the habit of addressing his ball and hitting it without a pause, a habit for which he would later become famous.

The boy also followed someone else around that summer — Stewart Maiden. Alex Smith, who was very active in competitive golf, had been succeeded in 1907 by his brother-in-law (also from Carnoustie, Scotland), Jimmy Maiden. The next year, Jimmy had hired his brother Stewart as assistant pro. After watching Stewart play several holes, the impressionable Bobby would head back to the thirteenth hole, near the Mule House. There he imitated Maiden's swing, pitching a capful of balls to the flagstick and putting them out, hour after hour. How well he imitated Stewart Maiden became apparent a few years later, as Bobby Jones relates in *Down the Fairway:*

> I was playing a practice round prior to the Southern Amateur Championship in Birmingham and this man, who had not seen Stewart since he left Carnoustie, was standing by Dad as I was driving off the tenth tee in the distance.
>
> 'When did Stewart Maiden get here?' he inquired.
>
> Dad told him that Stewart was not there at all.
>
> 'You can't fool me,' was the rejoinder. 'I saw Stewart drive just now from the tenth tee. Think I don't know that old Carnoustie swing?'

Bobby's version of that old Carnoustie swing began that summer in 1908, when the 6-year-old watched Maiden, quietly and intently, absorbing an extraordinary amount of information about stance and swing.

The relationship between Bobby and Stewart Maiden, who became club pro when his brother moved on, would develop into strong affection through the years. "Stewart was a real funny guy," Jones later observed to a *Club Times* reporter (September 1968). "He had a talent for making very pungent, irreverent, witty remarks and I remember several instances in which he commented on members in one way or another. Of one of them he said, not wholly seriously, 'Oh he's a great player. He has only one fault. He can't hole out soon enough.' " Jones added another anecdote about Maiden: "Once Stewart had been giving lessons to a club member for quite a while, and someone asked him how he was getting along with the guy. Maiden said in his rich, Scottish brogue, 'I can't do a thing for him — after five minutes he's teaching me.' "

Jones also recalled how the Scotsman favored the better players. "If you did not have any particular promise, he'd give you lessons all right, but he wouldn't take much interest in you." He illustrated with this story: "Another member, off his game, went out to take a lesson from the pro and he was asked to hit five or six balls, which he did. Then as he started to hit another, Stewart stepped up, grabbed him by the wrist and held him — he had a grip like iron — looked him straight in the eye and said, 'Damit, Red, do you *have* to play golf?'"

Young Bobby soon proved he was one of the players worth Stewart Maiden's notice. In 1911, at 9 years old he won a "real" cup, the City Junior Championship (which was played on the East Lake course), besting Howard Thorn, seven years his senior, by 5 and 4. His picture, alongside that of his large teenaged competitor, appeared in *The American Golfer.* Two years later, at 11, he won the club championship and held it for three years, long enough to earn a permanent trophy. It was a prize he had coveted since the competition began in 1907, when he was a 5-year-old in Mrs. Meador's boarding house.

Jones, age 9

Beginning at 6, Bobby Jones intently imitated the stance and swing of Stewart Maiden.

While athletes in other sports continued to excel at the Athletic Club, gradually golf began to outstrip other sports in popularity. And its popularity surged in 1913, when an unknown ex-caddie, Frances Ouimet, defeated the well-known British golfers, Ted Ray and Harry Vardon, to win the U. S. Open. The image of golf began to shift, with his victory, from being a sport for the wealthy to being an all-American sport. Says Herbert Wind, "Only twelve years after its introduction in Yonkers, golf had come to be regarded by Americans of that day more or less as . . . an outdoor recreation, open to both sexes and a wide range of ages,

Jones, age 14

16

whose environment was as attractive, if not more attractive, than the exercise itself; a sport whose first professionals came from overseas and whose leading missionaries were the college crowd, and which offered its followers an occasion for dashing outfits, endowed them with the bright aura of being fashionable, and demanded from them a good slice of their incomes."

This was a sport anyone had a chance to win, and more and more Americans tried their hand at it, in Atlanta as elsewhere. From 350,000 in 1913, the number of American golfers would swell to 2,000,000 within a decade.

Bobby, Perry, and Alexa

The trio of youngsters who had competed together in Frank Meador's tournament in 1908, just as other children might have joined in a neighborhood softball game, had begun to attract regional and even national attention by 1915. Tagging along behind their parents or behind Stewart Maiden,

they had learned the movements and language of golf as easily as they had learned English, and within a few years the club began to realize it had bred some unusual talent. Perry was the first to attract attention, winning not only local competitions but tournaments outside Atlanta.

Bobby, too, began to make his mark outside Atlanta. At 13, the youngest of the three, he created something of a sensation in the Southern Tournament, although he did not win. He then went on to win the Invitational Tournament at Cherokee Club in Knoxville and the Invitational at Birmingham Country Club. In his hometown that year he won the AAC and Druid Hills Club championships. And in 1916, a now-chubby 14-year-old, he knocked the socks off everyone at the Georgia State Amateur, held at the Capital City Club's new country club in Brookhaven. There he earned worldwide attention by defeating two former champions before being beaten on the third round.

A few weeks later 19-year-old Alexa outpaced both Bobby and Perry by capturing the Woman's

The combination of the youth and expertise of the "Dixie Kids" was irresistible to galleries. 1917-18: Perry Adair,

Alexa Stirling, Bob Jones, Elaine Rosenthal. Exhibition Matches for Red Cross — World War I.

17

Bobby Jones challenges Perry Adair's lead as the club's golf prodigy. (Bobby, second from left; Perry, third from left)

National Golf Championship at Belmont Springs Country Club (in Massachusetts) on October 7. *The Atlanta Journal* reported that day:

A large gallery had gathered for the event and trailed out behind the contestants over the links. Among the spectators today was Stewart Maiden, professional from the Atlanta Athletic Club East Lake course. Miss Stirling is a pupil of Maiden and the little Scot watched her play today closer probably than anyone else in the gallery. Mr. Maiden is also instructor to 'Little Bob' Jones and Perry Adair who were sensations in the men's national amateur championship last month. . . .

Miss Stirling has attracted far and away more attention than any other one candidate here, partly on account of her youth, but more because of her skill coupled with businesslike tactics in going after what she wants. . . .

Thus Stirling became AAC's first national golf champion. But not its last.

East Lake had been born at exactly the right time to nourish some undreamed-of talent. "I could at times even visualize another St. Andrews," Harry Atkinson later confided to O. B. Keeler, "but I never saw, even in the rosiest moments of the vision, an Alexa Stirling, a Bobby Jones, who were to carry East Lake to the top of the world as a home of golf. . . ."

18

Chapter Four

The Golden Golf Era

*P*erry Adair, three or four years older than Bobby Jones, had taken the lead as the club's golf prodigy. But in 1916, when he faced his friend Bobby in that Georgia State Championship, a turning point occurred in their relative roles. It was then that Bobby Jones first gave full vent to his competitive instincts and, in the metaphor of competitive sports, discovered the "lion" in his heart. Only then did he begin to realize the possible scope of his own talent. Jones later described that revelation in *Golf Is My Game:*

Up to this moment, despite the fact that I had won two out of the three matches in which Perry and I had met, I still considered that he was the better golfer. I looked up to him and thought that I had managed to win from him a couple of times mainly by accident. It was in this match at Brookhaven over thirty-six holes that I finally gained confidence in myself and my game.

In the morning round I think I must have been tense, overanxious, and perhaps a little bit resigned. At any rate I played some pretty sloppy golf and came in for lunch three down. While I was having a few practice putts prior to the start of the afternoon round, the tournament chairman came up to me and asked that I play out the bye holes, with the obvious inference that Perry would beat me several holes before the finish, and he wanted the gallery to have the privilege of seeing a full eighteen holes of play. I replied that I would, without calling his attention to what I considered to be a rather obvious and unpleasant implication. Nevertheless, it appeared that he was right when I began the afternoon round by hooking my tee shot out of bounds and losing the first hole with a scrambling six, thus becoming four down.

But at this point I remember to this day that my whole attitude changed completely. Instead of being on the defensive and uncertain, I began to play hard, aggressive golf, hitting the ball with all the force at my command and striving to win hole after hole, rather than to avoid mistakes.

After halving the short second hole in three,

I drove to the edge of the green on the third hole, something I had never done before, and from then on hit the ball as hard as I had ever hit it in my life. Perry played reasonably well, but he missed a couple of putts, notably on the eighth and tenth holes, and I finally won the match on the last green two up. I had played the eighteen holes in seventy, with the beginning six.

This was the match which gained for me my first opportunity to play in a National Championship, and also gave me what assurance I needed to enjoy taking advantage of it. I think what did most for me was Perry's remark as he put my ball into my hand on the last green. With understandable disregard for grammar, he had muttered, 'Bob, you are just the best.'

In hindsight, Adair's comment is poignant. The next 15 years would show that Bobby Jones was, indeed, the best — the best in the world. His skills, combined with the skills of his remarkably talented friends at East Lake, would make this a spectacularly exciting period for golf in his hometown. But first, Bobby had a few dues-paying years ahead of him.

The Dixie Kids

In keeping with that camaraderie, Perry's father invited Bobby to make the trip with them to Philadelphia to the United States Amateur in 1916. Sportswriter Herbert Wind describes what happened there:

When Bobby appeared at the Merion Cricket Club, in Ardmore, about ten miles from downtown Philadelphia, he was fourteen and a half, a chunky boy five-feet-four and weighing 165 pounds. Cocky as they came, too, not the least bit impressed by any of the names assembled for the meeting, and rather temperamental, to put it mildly. After a poor shot, the youngster threw clubs and recited some of the more fragrant cusswords he had learned on the back steps of the Jones house on Willow Street from the cook's brother. Bobby managed to qualify, and in the first round he was paired with Eben Byers, who threw a nice club himself. Bobby won a battle of tempers 3 and 1; Byers, Bobby used to explain in later years, ran out of clubs first. He moved along by defeating Frank Dyer 4 and 2 and came up against the defending champion, Bob Gardner, in the third round. Taking advantage of Jones' wildness and putting splendidly himself in the afternoon, Gardner stopped the kid on the 31st green, but not before he had been called on to play every bit of golf he knew. Jones was the sensation of the tournament. Everyone went home raving about the boy from Atlanta who hit the ball so naturally and hit it so perfectly in the bargain that, even at fourteen, he was one of the longest drivers in the field. Old Walter Travis, a tough man to please, was bowled over by the shots he had seen the youngster play. "Improvement?" snorted the Old Man when someone asked him about Jones' potential. "He can never improve his shots, if that's what you mean. But he will learn a good deal more about playing them."

The Athletic Club buzzed about the prospects for this youngster, and the next year he confirmed their expectations by winning the Southern title in a tournament in Birmingham.

With national interest focused on the trio of Jones, Stirling, and Adair, the three were an excellent fund-raising draw for the war effort when they went on a national Red Cross Tour in 1917 and 1918. Elaine Rosenthal, who was known as the best woman golfer in the Midwest, joined them. The combination of the youth and expertise of the four were irresistible to galleries. "The troupe usually played mixed four-ball matches," explains Wind. "One day Bobby would team up with Elaine, the next with Alexa. Now and then the girls would sit out a date and watch the Dixie Kids, Jones and Adair, fire away against players twice their age. No one who saw the kids ever forgot Alexa and Elaine clouting their mashies as naturally as most girls took to dancing, or Bobby and Perry wearing their red Swiss Guard berets and having the time of their lives making the hard game of golf look as easy as hopscotch."

The war over, Alexa took the national women's title again in 1919 and 1920. Meanwhile, Bobby won the Southern title again in 1920, and Perry won it (while Bobby was abroad) in 1921 and again in 1923.

The Runner-Up Years

The years immediately following the war were frustrating for Bobby, however. In 1919 he reached the finals of the U.S. Amateur, but lost to S. D. Herron. In 1920 he was eliminated in the semifinals by Francis Ouimet. And in his first venture into the U. S. Open he wound up four strokes behind the winner, Ted Ray of England. In 1921 he made

his first attempt at a British crown in the British Amateur, but lost in the fourth round to Allan Graham. He entered the British Open, but withdrew, discouraged with his performance. In the U.S. Open he finished four strokes behind the winner, Jim Barnes, and in the U.S. Amateur he lost to Willie Hunter in the third round. In 1922 he finished a painful one stroke off in the U.S. Open and lost to Jess Sweetser in the U.S. Amateur. After being heralded a boy wonder back in 1916, Jones had not managed to win a single national title in six years.

The frustration drove his well-known temper to the limits. But, to his credit, he finally outgrew his public outbursts. "Fortunately for Bobby, in the 1921 British Open he was guilty of an impetuous gesture of which he was so ashamed after he cooled down that, once and for all, he graduated from adolescence," explains Wind. "On his third round in the tournament, it had taken him 46 strokes to reach the turn. He was burning up. On the tenth, Bobby ran into a double-bogey 6, and when he had played five strokes on the short eleventh and was still not in the cup, he picked his ball up — the equivalent in golf of throwing in the towel. Bobby Jones had quit in competition. This, as he saw it, was an unforgivable breach of the sportsman's code, and the ever-rankling memory of what he had done on the eleventh at St. Andrews, as much as any single factor, was responsible for the magnificent standard of deportment Bobby Jones created in later years."

Kiltie the King-Maker

Sometime during this period Bobby went to his longtime mentor, Stewart Maiden, for help. Maiden, as usual, was at work on a set of golf clubs. Arch Martin remembers watching Maiden's craftsmanship: "It was so interesting to watch him fashion a golf club — either fashion a head of a driver and put the shaft on it or take an iron head and put a shaft in it. There was an art in it, and he knew it from the beginning. He used to take a rough hickory shaft and fashion that thing and shape it, reduce the size of it to give it a little 'whip,' as they called it. And he would use varnish and cottonseed oil and some ink black to bark the grain in the wood. Then he would polish it down to a very fine finish and then put on a leather grip in strips, twisting around and around to end the thing, then securing it at the end with a tack and some linen thread.... He kept a supply of ready-made clubs and people were continually breaking shafts, particularly our Bob Jones."

On this particular day, Jones was not looking for a club. He was looking for advice. "I had been having a most trying time with my long irons, and some sort of tournament was in the offing," he later recalled in *Golf Is My Game:*

I had tried to work the thing out for myself, but could not do so. There didn't seem to be any pattern to work on. I would hook a few and then hit one a mile out to the right. In desperation at last, I told Stewart of my troubles while he was at his bench planing down a hickory shaft.

At first he said nothing, which I had long before learned was a normal response for him. After a while, though, he took the club out of the vise, squeezed the grip end as no one else could ever do, so that a barely perceptible tremor agitated the whole club, appeared not wholly displeased and set it aside for further attention later on.

"Let's go," he said. With no more conversation my caddy, with my clubs, and I followed Stewart down the first fairway to a spot some two hundred yards from the green. "Hit a few," he said. I hit two. As I stepped up to the next, he said, "Wait." With the grip end of a club he was holding in his hands, he rapped quite sharply on my left arm just below the shoulder. I moved back. Again he rapped. "Move back," he said. I moved back some more, then looked up to see where I was aiming. "Stewart," I said, "I'll knock this ball into that left-hand bunker." "Never mind," he said, "back some more. Now, that's good." "What do I do now?" I asked, trying to be bitterly sarcastic. "Knock hell out of it," said Stewart. I did. The ball almost landed in the hole. I hit another and another straight at the flag. I looked up for Stewart, but he was on his way back to his shop to finish that club.

With his emotions under control and his skills honed to a fine pitch, Bobby was generally considered past due for a breakthrough into golf's big leagues.

Bobby Leaps to Fame

In 1923 Bobby, 21, gloriously broke out of his runner-up standing with a win in the U.S. Open at Inwood Country Club in Inwood, Long Island. "Bobbie Leaps to Fame" the Atlanta newspapers crowed in headlines, little suspecting the magnitude of achievements that lay ahead. In the 1924 U.S. Open he came in second, three strokes behind Cyril Walker, but won the U.S. Amateur.

The 1925 U.S. Amateur was the scene of something that was and remains unique in golfing. The two golfers who played in the finals for the championship were members of the same club, East Lake. One was Bobby Jones and the other was Watts Gunn.

While the trio of Adair, Stirling, and Jones had been making its mark, Watts Gunn had been steadily building his own achievements. Born in 1905 in Macon, Georgia, Gunn had not had the advantage of growing up near a golf course. But during the early twenties he developed his game while he was at Georgia Tech. He also became a member of AAC at that time.

By 1925 Gunn had become a remarkable golfer. And his showing in the U.S. Amateur that year was the stuff of legends. O. B. Keeler relates one of those legends in the October 1925 issue of *The American Golfer:*

Watts had shot the first nine holes against the Western Pennsylvania champion in a sorry 42, five strokes above par, and was two down. Then he started back 5-5, each a stroke above par, and lost another hole. Then, with a great chance to win the 621 yard twelfth, he had deftly steered his third shot into a trap.

Now it was at this precise moment, as near as I can make out, that Mr. Gunn was spiritually renovated or in some other manner made over from a nervous little neophyte sputtering shots about the scene of his first big championship, into a cold, precise, grim and implacable golfing machine clicking off pars and birdies to the utter destruction of Vincent Bradford and Jess Sweetser, and later, by a sort of reversion, giving Bobby Jones the hardest run he has had in two championships.

I recalled plainly that Watts had waded down into that trap by the twelfth green and blasted out in a shower of river sand less than a yard from the cup, and had rammed down the putt for a par and a win. And now he was off, on a record-setting spin of winning fifteen consecutive holes in a national championship.

It is easy enough to say that Bradford played bad golf — of course he did. But starting two up through No. 12, Vincent Bradford could have shot every hole of the next 14 in absolute par, and have been hauled back to square. Watts Gunn was simply beating the card; he had twelve holes in par and three birdies; and he missed a twelve foot putt at the sixteenth in the morning; a seven footer at the fifth in the afternoon; and a ten-footer on the 253-yard eighth hole, the last of the match, for other birdies which he might as well have had, though par was good enough to win them.

It was as perfect an exhibition of flawless, mechanical golf as ever was seen; two putts from a moderate distance for every par; never a shot off line; never an effort for a par; but always just missing — or getting — the birdies.

"Were you scared," I asked, "when you started your next match with Jess Sweetser?"

"Scared?" he said. "I was scared stiff. I was so scared I was numb. I was glad I was numb, because it sort of kept me from suffering so much."

In this numb condition, Watts shot the first nine holes (against Sweetser) in par 37, and turned 3 up, and then played the last nine in 34, just as Bobby Jones had played the second nine in 34 against Sweetser in 1922. But where Bobby went in to lunch 5 down, Watts walked

Continued on page 26

*The gallery
holds its breath with Jones
in the 1929 U.S. Open. Jones won.*

Bobby Jones displays his form at 23.

Bobby Jones — nothing could stop him now!

Jones proudly holds his young son.

Jones receives accolades for the Grand Slam with an expression of vague uneasiness — like a boy who would like nothing better than to be allowed to go home. Robert

T. Jones, Jr., Mrs. Robert T. Jones, Jr., and Robert P. Jones — 1930.

Jones gets a congratulatory handshake from veteran
Tris Speaker.

Jones became a symbol
of the model American athlete.

*Replicas of
the Grand Slam
trophies: British Open,
U.S. Amateur, British
Amateur, U.S. Open.*

For my Mother and Dad,
With devoted love,
Rob

To Colonel and Mrs. Robert P. Jones
with best wishes from
their friend
Dwight D. Eisenhower

*A print of the
portrait of Bobby Jones
painted by President
Dwight D. Eisenhower,
which hangs in the Bobby
Jones Room at the
Atlanta Athletic Club.*

off the eighteenth green in the astonishing position of 7 up.

I walked off the green with him, an arm across his sweating shoulders, and asked, "How do you feel now?"

"Gee," he said, "I'm hungry. I'm so hungry, my pants are about to fall off."

Then he proceeded to abate that peril, in utter defiance of my suggestion that championships are won on toast and tea.

When Watts and Jess took the first tee for the afternoon round, Watts' run from that blast out of the No. 12 trap had extended to 33 holes in four strokes under par, of which he had won 24 and lost only two. In the matinee round, he did not give Jess a chance, shooting every hole exactly in par except the 9th, where he ended the match with a birdie 4, for one of the most flawless exhibitions ever seen in championship golf.

That was the kind of performance Bobby Jones was up against when he met Gunn in the finals.

Charles Elliott describes the meeting of these two tough competitors at Oakmont:

Both were playing superb golf and when they came to what Bob termed the "ghost hole" because the blast of a nearby megaphone had cost him the hole and a match with Davy Herron six years before, Gunn at 2 under par had Jones one up in the Amateur finals, and was playing what Bob termed "the hottest inspirational golf I ever faced."

The "ghost hole" was a 600-yarder. Gunn was comfortably on in three, but Jones' third shot found the bunker. He felt that if he lost that hole, he would never again catch Gunn. Bob blasted out of the trap to within 10 feet of the cup and sank his putt for a par to halve the hole.

"That set him on fire," Watts recalled. "Jeepers! From there in I shot the best golf I knew how to shoot, but you know what I faced? He showed me a 3-3-4-3-3-4 and at the end of the first eighteen holes I was four down. When he started the afternoon round at 4-3, it cooked my goose. I never caught up."

The fine performance of his fellow club member had fired up Jones' competitive instincts, as had the performance of Perry Adair some years earlier.

Bobby Jones was now on a winning streak. In 1926 he won the U. S. Open and the British Open and was runner-up in the U.S. Amateur; in 1927 he won the U.S. Amateur and the British Open; in 1928 he won the U.S. Amateur and came in second in the U.S. Open; and in 1929 he won the U.S. Open.

The Grand Slam

Jones had become a national figure who attracted thousands of worshipping fans at every appearance. In the handsome figure he now cut and in his modest and courteous deportment, he commanded a devotion from fans that was matched only by the worship accorded that other American hero of the 1920s, Charles Lindbergh, also handsome and also outwardly controlled and modest. When Lindbergh visited Atlanta after his long-distance aviation feat the adoring city renamed a street for him. And when Bobby Jones returned home from his victory at St. Andrews the same year, Atlantans called him the "Lindbergh of golf." Herbert Wind described his charisma with the public: "The American sports public didn't know the intimate personal habits of Jones, but what they saw of him was an accurate index of the man. They liked the way he acted in competition. They liked the way he looked —clean-cut, boyish and grown-up at the same time. A decade or so before they had flocked to Ouimet because he was a young American they understood and admired, and it may not be at all excessive to say that they worshipped Jones, and formed an enduring enthusiasm for the game he played, because of all the heroes in the Golden Age of Sport, he stood forth as the model American athlete."

This was a hero who would not disappoint his fans. In 1930, as Atlanta and the world hung on his every movement, he climbed his way, one match after another, to the pinnacle in golfing: first the British Amateur; then the British Open; then the British Open; then the U.S. Open; and, finally the U.S. Amateur. He had done it! He had won the Grand Slam, one of the greatest feats in sporting history.

His country and his city resounded with praise as the titles accumulated in 1930. The first celebration came when Jones returned to the United States on July 2, 1930, after winning the two British crowns. He arrived on board the ship *Europa* and was taken on an official tug into the city, with the steamer *Mandalay* escorting him, 200 Georgians, aboard. AAC member Alva Maxwell was one of those Georgians who had traveled to New York to welcome their hometown hero. "I shall never forget the tremendous crowd who gathered on Broadway and the tons of confetti and torn paper which were thrown from buildings in his honor. . . . George Sargent has said many times that Bob Jones has made East Lake the best known golf course in the world, with the possible exception of St. Andrews."

A scant two weeks later Jones had captured his third title for the year, the U.S. Open, at Interlachen Country Club in Edina, Minnesota. This time it was Atlanta that threw the celebration.

AAC member Ralph Williams remembers the occasion: "The club hired a big double-deck bus, and I was on top of that bus. We went down to the railroad station to meet him and we were in the parade." As Jones sat in the reviewing stand and waved, practically every civic and social organization in the city passed in parade and cheered: police, firemen, Chamber of Commerce delegates, Kiwanians, Civitans, Rotarians, an American Legion corps, the Atlanta Crackers baseball team, Georgia Tech alumni, Georgia Power Company employees, the Atlanta Athletic Club, the AAC basketball team, and representatives of the city's other downtown and country clubs. Favorites with the crowd were a contingent of 300 caddies from all the clubs.

Bobby Jones shouldered all this attention with an expression of vague uneasiness, like a boy who would like nothing better than to be allowed to just go home. "For a man who exerted so compelling a magnetism over American sports fans, Jones was an exceptionally restrained performer," says Herbert Wind. "He did not dramatize himself like Tilden or Hagen. He made no appeal to primitive human emotions, like Dempsey. He was no happy extrovert like Ruth. Jones' stupendous popularity — unprecedented in what had been a minor sport until he emerged — rested partially on a skill so apparent that it needed no showboating, and partially on the type of man he was."

Jones completed the Grand Slam in September by winning the U.S. Amateur at the Merion Cricket Club near Philadelphia. To his relief, he found that no large celebration was planned. As he rode into Peachtree Station by train, hundreds of friends and fans welcomed him informally. For Jones, that was the best kind of celebration. "Charlie, I really like people, believe it or not I do," he confided to Charles Yates in later years. "But I like them best in small doses."

Although every fan who met Jones at Peachtree Station that day was inspired by his achievement, it was the golfers among them who really understood the depth of it. Herbert Wind captures the emotion many of them felt as they welcomed home the world's greatest golfer:

> There was a clear, cold aesthetic thrill in watching Jones hit a golf ball. The other leading players had excellent form that a duffer could appreciate, and they got results that spoke for themselves. Compared to Jones, though, they didn't look so finished. You noticed a little bumpiness in their backswing, a vague departure from the blueprint at impact, the expenditure of brute force in the followthrough. You looked at Jones and you saw the copybook form that you and two million other American golfers were striving for. You saw a one-piece swing in which the man had somehow incorporated every 'must' your pro had enumerated — the left arm straight but not rigid on the backswing; the weight shifted from left to right going back and then gradually returned to the left side again as the club started down and the hands moved into position to unleash their power; the hit *through* the ball; the finish with the weight entirely transferred to the left side and the hands high — the million other integrated contributions of the chin, the hips, the balls of the feet, the knees, the grip, the left shoulder, the right ankle, the wrists, the eyes. If you could buckle down and remember to do all those things, then you, too, would play like Jones. No, you couldn't at that. You would always lack that something which lifted Jones above mechanical perfection. It was hard to put your finger on it. It had to do with a certain *je ne sais quoi* quality that made Bobby's swing so rhythmically singular, made it appear so effortless though you knew it was built on effort. Bernard Darwin came as close as anyone to tagging the genius of Jones when he said, without any gingerbread, that there was a strain of poetry in Bobby.

This really was the best kind of celebration for an athlete — a celebration by people who understood what he had accomplished.

Atlanta, Golfing Capital

With Bobby Jones' fame came fame for Atlanta as a golfing center and particularly for East Lake Country Club. Since 1915 Atlantans had held at least one major golfing title, between Bobby Jones, Perry Adair, Alexa Stirling, Helen Lowndes, and Margaret Maddox.

To support the wide interest in golf that had been generated since the founding of East Lake Country Club, courses had been built at Druid Hills Golf Club, Capital City Country Club, Ingleside Country Club, Ansley Park Golf Club, and West End Golf Club, in addition to six public and semi-public courses, including the new Bobby Jones Municipal Course. It was the golden age of golfing for Atlanta. And East Lake, gloriously, was its center.

The Atlanta Athletic Club had been privileged. The particular time in history, the country club facility, and the talent had all come together to produce something special in athletics: a champion without peer anywhere in the world. The vision of George Adair, of Harry Atkinson, and of countless AAC members had not only been realized. It had been far surpassed.

Chapter Five

More Than Bricks and Mortar

*I*n the years when Bobby Jones was conquering both his own temperament and the demands of the game to ascend to the peak of golfing fame, the Atlanta Athletic Club demonstrated its own resiliency and determination in the face of adversity.

It was a time when fires were common and the resources to fight fires were often inadequate. That left the city's residents and their institutions vulnerable to dramatic and unexpected losses. The Piedmont Driving Club, for example, burned in 1906 (and was rebuilt the following year). In 1908 fire destroyed 30 buildings in the western quarter of the business district. And in 1917 a searing wall of blazes engulfed 1,938 houses over an area of 300 acres in a single day.

The Athletic Club was not to escape this dreaded phenomenon of the time. It was struck by two disastrous fires within little more than a decade. Both came at a time when the club had already extended itself financially to improve the golf course.

Fire Strikes East Lake

The first fire came at the onset of an ambitious project — the restructuring of the golf course. Bendelow's layout, a backward layout popular at the time (progressing clockwise), had earned a mixed reception. "That first course was a sort of strange layout as golf courses go, because it had only two 3-par holes, the first and the third," said Bobby Jones in later years. "The second was a par 4½. Yes, 4½ — too tough for a par 4 and not tough enough for a par 5." In a June 3, 1938, article in *The Atlanta Constitution*, Jones' friend, O. B. Keeler, commented on the remaining holes. "After you got past the third," he wrote, "you faced an interminable vista of good, hard slugging, or at least slugging."

Some of the toughest holes earned nicknames, according to Jones. "A couple I recall were the sixteenth, that we knew as the 'circus ring' because of its appearance, and the fourteenth, where you had to play a shot around or over the 'spectacle bunker' — a double trap that was, of course, shaped like a pair of eyeglasses."

Though they viewed the unusual course with affectionate humor, the club's golfers were generally agreed there must be a better way to lay it out. In 1913 George Adair, his son Perry, and Stewart Maiden made a trip to Scotland to see other possible course layouts; when they returned Adair proposed that the course be rearranged so that each nine ended at the clubhouse. The board accepted the proposal and selected golf course architect Donald Ross to accomplish the change.

Fire called an abrupt halt to the work on March 22, 1914, completely destroying the clubhouse. Immediately, the membership contracted to build another — and larger — clubhouse, with Walter Danning as architect. The structure was financed by issuing 25-year, 6 percent interest bonds, to be paid in gold coins, giving the club a bonded indebtedness of about $180,000.

Both the new clubhouse and the rearranged course were formally opened on July 4, 1915. Longtime member Arch Martin, who joined in 1915, recalls what the new clubhouse looked like: "The clubhouse was a great big frame building with a screen porch all around it and rocking chairs all over the place. It was a delightful place with a ballroom on the first floor and maybe some private dining rooms, and the men's locker room and the ladies' locker room. As I recall, the men's locker room was in the basement of the first floor. And the golf shop was in the basement."

The new clubhouse and particularly the "new" course were extremely popular. The residential community around East Lake was gradually growing, spurred by real estate developers such as George Adair. and with downtown Atlanta continuing to grow, East Lake Country Club became a favorite country retreat from the noise of the city. "The club has now a membership of 1,000, with a large waiting list," reported the *Atlanta Journal Magazine* on January 4, 1914. "Its income amounts to several hundred thousand dollars a year, and it is probably the richest social club in the city."

Champions

As the second decade of the century arrived, golf, tennis, and basketball attracted the lion's share of participation and press coverage for the Athletic Club. Bobby Jones was just reaching national prominence at the time, Carleton Smith was dominating Southern singles tennis, and Bean's Boys were consistently netting wins in Southern basketball tournaments. But swimming, too, was a popular sport during this period. Swimming competitions were held in the lake over a course Bobby Jones defined as "from the old poplar tree where we used to find bream beds just opposite the dining room, up to the bridge." It proved to be a worthy course. In 1921 the club's team won the Southern AAU Swimming Championship. The team included Tom Cureton, Bud Glenn, Gilbert Fraser, Ed Hatcher, Phil Schoeneck, M. M. "Scrappy" O'Sullivan, Steve Hartner, Bill Noyes, Bernard Neal, and Melton Coleman.

These swimmers, and others who joined them, continued to score wins for the club in city, regional, and even national meets. On August 8, 1926, the *Atlanta Journal Magazine* reported, "Perhaps no club ever produced as many fine swimmers as East Lake. There are far too many to mention, but among the best known divers are Steve Hartner, 'Scrappy' O'Sullivan, and Bill Murray. Virginia Ashe leads women swimmers, not only in the south, but ranks among the best in the country. Ed Hatcher, Bill Young, 'Red' Holloman and many others [such as Gilbert Fraser, Homer Thompson, and Mariana Goldsmith] are human fish when they don bathing suits. E. Lambert, the life guard, says that children seem to learn to swim almost as easily as they learn to walk at East Lake, because they are all so crazy about the water."

On the club's 25th anniversary in 1923, the May 6 *Atlanta Journal Magazine* summed up its remarkable achievements in athletics: "On August 15 the Atlanta Athletic Club will celebrate its silver anniversary. During its life it has made the record of having produced more champions in more different lines of sports than any other southern club.

"In golf, tennis, baseball, basketball, swimming and track, the club has captured titles, earned victories and made records. In 25 years it has grown from a little club of 65 men to a club of 1,700 members, a country club that is one of the most attractive in existence, a golf course that ranks with the best in the United States, and a waiting list nearly half as large as the membership."

Another Clubhouse for East Lake

On November 22, 1925, fire struck again at East Lake. Once again, the clubhouse was destroyed.

Lost in the fire this time was Bobby Jones' U.S. Amateur trophy, won in his final round against Watts Gunn and displayed in the club's main lobby.

For the second time — this time under the leadership of President Scott Hudson — the membership at once made plans not only to rebuild, but to build even larger quarters. The result was a spacious clubhouse of 3 stories, designed by Hertz, Reid & Adler, with more dining space and a large locker room for men on the second floor. While the club was being built, the members retreated to their original quarters at East Lake — the bath- and boathouse — where lockers were installed until the clubhouse could be completed.

When the new clubhouse was opened in August 1926, it was a stunning sight, an elegant Tudor-style structure set in 200 acres of rolling golf course. The interior was described in detail by Medora Perkerson in the *Atlanta Journal Magazine* of August 8, 1926:

> The interior is Georgian, more restrained and formal in treatment than that of the club replaced, yet achieving a homelike atmosphere which is the charm of the Georgian manner truly expressed. The fireplaces in dining room and lounges, around which so many pleasant groups have gathered, lost a little of their feudal proportions in the rebuilding, but they have gained a more classic beauty of outline. Anyway, they are still large enough to accommodate the huge logs piled down near the caddy house. . . .
>
> The main lounge is now one of the largest clubrooms in the country. The great stair which formerly dominated the room has been replaced by a graceful flight half hidden at one end. There is a private salon for small parties, and opening off the main lounge on all three sides is an immense porch, with cloister-like columns, an ideal setting for afternoon affairs. This porch, at least three times as large as the one replaced, overlooks the terrace at the back, which on Saturday evenings, with its demicircle of tables, colored lights and gay dancers, presents a scene of fairy-like beauty. Beyond, is the formal garden, which finally loses itself in the lake. In addition to the Saturday night dinner dances, the club will inaugurate Sunday evening concert dinners, the same as those given at the town club, offering two happy solutions for the Sunday night supper problem.

After almost a year without a country club, the members were elated to have the club back in full operation.

As a housewarming, the members had an exciting event to celebrate: the conquest by Bobby Jones of the British Open, the first time it had been won by an amateur in 29 years and the first time ever by an American. Members of the Piedmont Driving Club, the Capital City Club, and the Druid Hills Golf Club were invited to join in the celebration, which was held in the ballroom of the new clubhouse at East Lake. The modest young hero was presented with a gift of a 3-carat diamond ring by his home club. On display was a new solid gold replica of the U.S. Amateur trophy that had been destroyed in the fire, and in its company were the new trophy for the British Open; the U.S. Open Cup that Bobby had won earlier that year; and the Walker Cup, which he had earned with his fellow member Watts Gunn.

A Few Favorites

With the opening of the new clubhouse, the members were pleased to see the longtime staff members return: J. K. Davenport as superintendent of the staff of 40, Fred Green as assistant, waiters known only as Harry and Davis, Walter in the men's locker room, and Bradley and Annie at the bathhouse. Annie in particular had gained the affection of club members as she chastened her 4- and 5-year-old charges into proper behavior.

Under the management of W. E. Richardson, who also managed the town club, the membership voted its approval of the new facilities by using them more than ever. Richardson had managed both the Capital City Club and the Piedmont Driving Club before coming to the Athletic Club in 1926 and brought with him a reputation for good management. "Little girls, now prominent society matrons, have grown up, had their debut parties and wedding receptions under Mr. Richardson's careful supervision," wrote Perkerson in the same *Atlanta Journal Magazine* article. "His experience, his executive ability and his genius for successful entertaining are an invaluable asset to any organization."

The Saturday night dances on the terrace were particularly popular, especially with the younger members: "We went out there every Saturday night," says Ralph Williams, who attended Tech High with Richardson's son Nolan. "It was a beautiful setting overlooking the lake — moonlight, a circular floor. Everyone was dressed up. There was a nice orchestra [such as Dean Hudson, Nu Nu Chastain, and Kay Kaiser]. . . . Sometimes they had a hard time getting everyone to leave when they closed at 12:00."

The Number Two Course

The increasing popularity of the club was nowhere more apparent than on the golf links. By the late 1920s golf had surpassed swimming and tennis

in popularity, with more than 500 members using the redesigned course. In good weather, especially on weekends, the course was packed. After a year or more of crowded conditions, the golfing members decided to look into a second course.

The most attractive location was directly across Second Avenue from the club's existing property, where a large, wooded tract lay behind a row of houses and building lots. After some debate on the

East Lake Country Club opened its elegant rebuilt clubhouse in 1926, after fire destroyed the earlier structure.

matter, given the recent outlay for the new clubhouse, the board decided to go ahead with the project. The club acquired the land in 1928 and turned again to Donald Ross to lay out the course, which would always be known as the "Number Two Course."

As the popularity of the new facilities became apparent, Richardson transferred George Bell, manager at the downtown facility, to East Lake in 1926 to handle the large crowds for meals, dances,

31

and other social functions. (Bell would remain at East Lake for 14 years.) Bell, in turn, tapped another resource from the downtown club — David Gartrell Williams (who had been employed by the club since 1924) — to handle the increased activity in the locker rooms.

Williams' outgoing personality and loyalty to the club's members quickly won him a place in their affections and eventually in the folklore of the club. "To the 500 or more golfers who play a reasonable number of rounds over our two courses each year, Dave represents the 19th hole, the relaxation around the table when the woods and irons and putter have been tucked away in their bags for another day," said the *Club Times* in later years (August 1, 1960). "He's the nursemaid, bartender, shoeshiner, matchmaker, attentive listener, gambler (but never more than a Coke or two on some hot big-league baseball game he has tuned in on his back room radio), and friend."

The *Club Times* also related a story that was often told about Dave. According to the story, one of his golfing regulars showed up on a Monday afternoon to play a round of golf with his preacher. When the member noticed that his golf shoes were missing from the top of his locker he asked Williams about them. "Don't you remember?" Williams reminded him. "It rained yesterday and they were so soaking wet that we kept them in the back room to dry."

Both the member and the preacher stared at him for a moment in silence — all it took for Williams to catch himself and improvise, "I mean, sir, it rained Saturday."

"I know what you mean," the preacher said dryly.

Williams' earnestness in caring for members' shoes was the subject of many stories. Once Bobby Jones reportedly asked him how things were going and Williams replied, "Mr. Jones, we're just having a terrible time. We can't keep up with shining shoes. I believe so many of them play golf out here just to get their shoes shined." Subsequently, whenever Jones hit a bad shot he was likely to smile and say, "Well, I just came out here to get my shoes shined."

In the custom of the day, members showed their affection for David Williams by bringing him their old clothes, shoes, and hats. It was during one of those moments that a member discovered how much he didn't know about the longtime employee. After loading Williams' arms with suits and shirts, the member asked, "What's the matter, Dave? You look worried."

"I am," Williams replied.

"What's the matter?"

"At one of my apartment houses," Williams

View of East Lake grounds after clubhous

Front view of the rebuilt clubhouse.

As locker room attendant at East Lake, David Gartrell Williams gradually became a part of the club's folklore.

(top, center) was rebuilt in the 1920's.

Side view of clubhouse (after it was rebuilt in 1926) from across bridge.

said, "the furnace ain't working right, and we're having a hard time trying to get it fixed."

The member spread the word about Williams' real estate holdings, and when Dave Williams retired from the Club in the late 1960s, after more than 40 years with the club, he had won not only the affection of the members, but also their respect for his business sense as well.

The Spirit Survives

Not even the repeated disasters of the fires at East Lake could daunt the spirit of the Athletic Club during this period. This was an organization of more than bricks and mortar. And, though both were overwhelmingly popular, it was an organization of more than Bobby Jones and golf. Like other citizens of Atlanta, the members continued to display the spirit of growth and optimism that had been apparent from the time of Burton Smith.

Atlanta continued to be a city of progress, with the ever-spreading commercial area and the ever-more-popular automobile pushing outward the residential areas of the city. The Georgian Terrace hotel at Ponce de Leon Avenue and Peachtree Street opened in 1912, a symbol of the expansion of the city northward. And the Ford Motor Company opened an assembly plant in Atlanta for Model Ts in 1915.

World War I, which sealed off the overseas markets for cotton, slowed the economic progress of the South for a brief period, but Atlanta quickly recovered its impetus. The first radio stations, WSB and WGST, came on the air in 1922; Hartsfield Airport (then Candler) opened in 1925; and in 1926 the newly established High Museum and Atlanta Historical Society provided a stronger cultural foundation for the city.

The Athletic Club was determined to remain a part of Atlanta's progress. Buckboards had become an anachronism, but high spirits apparently had not.

Chapter Six

A Grand Club on Carnegie Way

$\mathcal{E}$ven while flames swept through the East Lake clubhouse in November 1925, a symbol of the club's vitality was slowly rising on a city block downtown. The new structure was the Carnegie Way town club.

A "Splendid New Building"

Though the Atlanta Athletic Club's country club had been immediately popular, it had drained away none of the interest in the downtown club. By 1919, with well above 1,000 members, the club had again outgrown the downtown facility and began to talk of enlarging the Auburn clubhouse or building an entirely new one.

This time the members discussed and researched the idea thoroughly over several years, collecting data on every athletic club of importance in the country. After exploring the possibility of another location, they settled on the site of the Lyric Theatre (originally a Vaudeville theatre), on the block bounded by Carnegie Way, Cone Street, and Williams Street (then James Street). In late 1924 the club decided to purchase the property from the Atlanta Theatre Company for a total of $275,000. The cash downpayment of $175,000 was generated through a second mortgage on the East Lake property.

That done, the building committee, consisting of President Scott Hudson and Athletic Committee Chairman Al Doonan, made a tour of the larger clubs in the Northeast to study their layouts and equipment. They were joined by Phil Shutze, a well-known Atlanta architect who had been commissioned to design the building.

The resulting structure, a 10-story, Georgian-style brick building, drew the immediate admiration of the public: "This new project has been by no means a secret," reported *The City Builder* in December 1925, "but the general public was not quite prepared for the structure that has almost suddenly made its appearance in the heart of downtown Atlanta. The building has now reached such a stage that a definite idea can be had as to

In 1926 the club opened a town club on Carnegie Way that Margaret Mitchell described as "magnificent."

The club's tiled pool was located at the rear of the building, on the former site of the Lyric Theatre.

The barber shop in the Carnegie Way club was one of many conveniences the new building offered members.

just what the interior of the Club will be, and those who have inspected it have been amazed."

One of those to inspect the new club was Margaret Mitchell, later to win worldwide fame as author of *Gone With the Wind*. At that time a writer for the *Atlanta Journal Magazine* and known as "Peggy" Mitchell, she gave a glowing account of the new club on April 4, 1926:

> To describe as magnificent the new home of the Atlanta Athletic Club, which is being completed at a cost of a million and a quarter dollars on the site of the old Lyric Theater at Carnegie Way and Cone streets, is to tell only half the story of this splendid new building. It is magnificent in furnishings and appointments, in beauty of design, in the luxuriousness of its velvet rugs, its red and gold damask draperies, and its elaborately-carved panelling.
>
> But almost immediately this first impression is crowded out by the thought of the completeness of its equipment for physical development, recreation and sports, its great tiled swimming pool, its squash tennis courts, its handball courts, its gymnasium with a seating capacity for 2,000 spectators for the club's basket ball and other games, its locker rooms for club members, for the club's teams and for visiting teams, its women's locker room and showers, its boys' locker room and showers, its business men's locker room, showers and special gymnasium; its wrestling room, its boxing room, its bridge room, its billiard room and its Turkish bath with various attendant rooms, steam room, dry heat room, needle shower room, electric cabinet 'baking out' room, massage room, barber shop, and, in fact, practically everything that would appeal to this side of the masculine nature.
>
> When the new Athletic club first throws open its doors, probably around June 1, the dreams of its members will be realized and Atlanta will have one of the finest buildings of its kind in the United States. There are larger clubhouses — though this one rises eleven stories to [including] the roof garden — but there are none finer and none more elaborately or more completely equipped.

However profuse Peggy Mitchell's praise might appear by today's journalistic standards, there was no doubt this was a grand club — the grandest Atlanta had ever known.

The first five floors were the setting for most of the athletic and social activities. The athletic facilities were located in the rear of the building on the first three floors. On the third floor there was also a stag facility, with a men's grill room, a

With the opening of the new town club, more children of both sexes began to participate in the athletic program.

The top four floors of the club were guest quarters, which the club operated like hotel rooms.

The men's grill, on the third floor, was a popular gathering place. The slot machines (left rear) were a strong source of revenues in the 1940's.

billiard room, and a bridge room. These quarters would later give rise to the term, "The Third Floor Boys." Remembered Bill Street fondly, "That's where most of the old members stayed. They had an open poker game there, and it went along all day long, right up to the closing time at night. Some of them used to play every day." (The club would later add slot machines to the stag floor, a strong source of revenues in their time.) Ladies' private dining rooms were on the fourth floor, and the fifth floor contained the "Crystal Room," the main dining room — two stories high and running the entire hundred-foot length of the building on its Carnegie Way side. This room would be remembered for decades for its grandeur, epitomized by three large, cut glass chandeliers reflecting on the gleaming terrazzo floors.

The sixth floor contained the business offices, and the top four floors were guest quarters, which the club operated like hotel quarters. They were rented to guests of members, both as a convenience and as a way to cover the facility's overhead. Each of the 60 rooms not only had a shower but a bathtub as well, and — the latest innovation — running ice water. Among the prominent Atlantans who would live at the Athletic Club at one time or another were Tom C. Law of the Law Chemical Company; Richard Higby, remembered as a fine golfer; H. B. Nicholson, chairman of the Coca-Cola Company at one time; and J. W. Jones, who moved to Atlanta in 1947 to become secretary to Robert W. Woodruff, president of the Coca-Cola Company.

Jones remembers what the rooms were like: "It was a conventional hotel-room size with the bath. One feature — this was pre-air-conditioning — was that in addition to the regular solid door there was a latticework half-door. You could lock the lattice door and leave the door open and get some air. It served the purpose very well." Guests were provided with room service and with three meals a day in the dining room.

On top of the building, aloof from the noise of the growing city but with an excellent view of it, was the roof garden, complete with dance floor.

The Sounds of Success

Never had life looked sweeter for a club than it did when the Carnegie Way club opened on June 15. Scott Hudson sat at a banquet table sparkling with crystal and silver, listening to the warm praise of fellow members who understood the role he had played in bringing this new town club into being. That very day he had also received a cable that Bobby Jones had won the British Open for the first time. Members chatted excitedly in small groups, and a deep sense of satisfaction colored the evening.

The "Crystal Room," the main dining room, was two stories high and ran the entire length of the building.

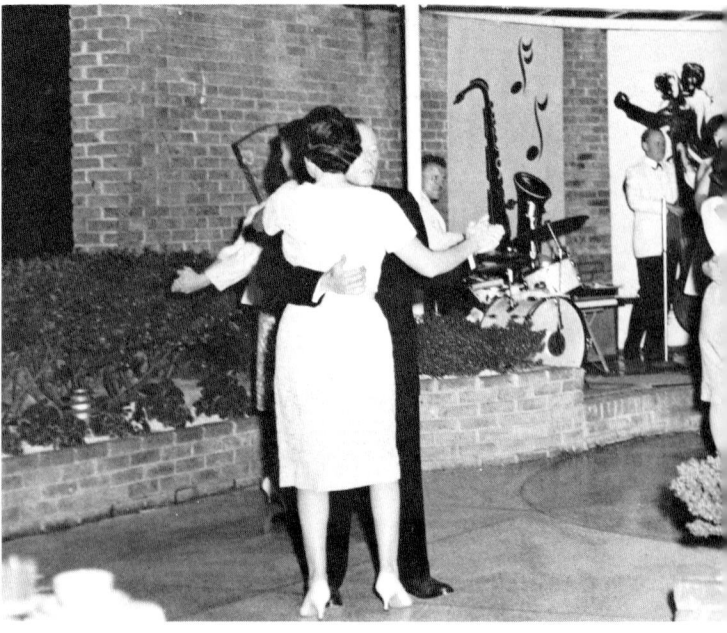

The roof garden of the new town club became one of the city's favorite spots for dancing.

38

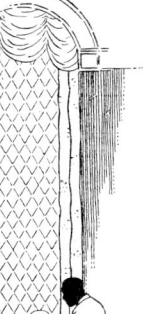

Atlanta
Athletic
Club

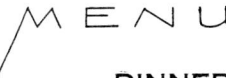

MENU

DINNER
6 to 9 p.m
$1.50

Canape Anchovies

Creole Gumbo   Hot or Cold Consomme

Crest Celery   Stuffed Olives

Broiled River Shad a la Princess
Scrambled Eggs with Chicken Livers on Toast
Fried Kentucky Ham Red Gravy
Broiled Lamb Chops Parsley Butter

Fried Egg Plant   Carrots and Peas
Chateau Potatoes

Asparagras Tips Salad
CHOICE OF
Strawberries a la Mode   Fresh Fruit Parfait
Fresh Strawberry Ice Cream   Vanilla or Chocolate Ice Cream **with cake**
or Fresh Fruit Sherbert with cake
Assorted Bread and Rolls   Coffee   Tea   Milk   Buttermilk

SPECIAL STEAK DINNER A A C $1.75

Canape Anchovies

Consomme en Tasse   ~~Creole Gumbo~~

Radishes   Spring Onions

Sirloin Steak a la Minute

Broiled Squab Chicken **Maitre d' Hotel**

Golden Yams   Carrots and Peas   **Fried Egg Plant**

Pineapple and Cheese Salad
CHOICE OF
Charlotte Russe   Strawberries in Cream
Fresh Strawberry Ice Cream   Vaniila or Chocolate Ice Cream with Cake
or Fresh Fruit Sherbert with cake
Assorted Bread   Hot Rolls   Coffee   Tea   Milk   Buttermilk

The 1929 menu from the Crystal Room.

Crystal Room in 1966, with dance floor on one end.

The athletic facilities at Carnegie Way resounded with the noises of tough competitive play. (L — R, rear: Marshall Clark, David Austin, Tommy Bates, Jimmy George, Jimmy Fischer, Dick Edwards. 2nd Row: Bob Allen, Reid Hartsfield, Bobby Pierce, Ronnie Straughan. Kneeling: Donald O'Brien, Bobby Boylston, recently named Athlete of the Month because of his participation as umpire in the 1987 Super Bowl.)

The club's gymnasium seated 2,000 spectators for basketball games and, in other seasons, was the setting for dinners and annual meetings.

Billiard champs receive their trophies.

The excitement of members about the new Carnegie Way facility spilled over into every activity the club offered. "The club was great for downtown business people. It was kind of like a hotel really," said Bill Street. "But, of course, everyone knew you." The numerous dining rooms on the fourth and fifth floors were often filled to capacity, and the roof garden became a favorite gathering place. "In the twenties, tea dances became more and more popular," writes Yolande Gwin in *Yolande's Atlanta.* "The Atlanta Biltmore Hotel inaugurated a weekly series, and many private clubs began the custom. Dining and dancing on the roof gardens of the Capital City Club and the Atlanta Athletic Club attracted society during the hot summer months."

Meanwhile, the athletic facilities below resounded with the noises of tough competitive play and frequent classes. "Bean's Boys," the rough-edged basketball team that had its start under Heisman and the hoops on Auburn Avenue, reveled in their new quarters. For the first time, they had seating for spectators. From 1925 through 1930, a more orthodox and polished team, Bean's almost unbeatable boys produced a record of 64 wins out of 74 games.

The nature of athletic interest at the club was gradually changing, however. Interest in team sports was generally declining, while individual sports were increasing in popularity, particularly with the new facilities for track, squash, and other forms of exercise and with the locker facilities for women and children. "Athletic clubs used to be built for men only," pointed out *The City Builder* in December 1925, when the Carnegie Way club was being built, "but with the forward march that the ladies have made, they have also become a necessary part of such institutions. Recognizing this fact, the designers of this new club have made ample provision for them. Some of the staid old members of the club are accepting this idea with a great deal of misgivings, but the arrangements are such that there will be absolutely no conflict, and the men can enjoy all privileges of the club with even more relaxation and freedom than has been the case in the old club."

Faith in the Future

The year 1926 has never been equalled in the club's history for optimism, solidarity, and achievement. Secure in its faith in the city's growth and its own future, the Athletic Club not only built a showplace for its downtown facility, but in the same summer opened its new Tudor clubhouse and its second 18-hole golf course at East Lake. "Thus two of the finest new clubs in the south were opened within two months of each other by one organization, the Atlanta Athletic club," wrote Medora Perkerson in the *Atlanta Journal Magazine* on August 8, 1926, "representing in buildings, property and equipment a combined total of approximately two million dollars."

This high level of investment in club life by the Atlanta Athletic Club was echoed in other cities in the United States during the "Roaring Twenties." "The clubhouse had now become the center of the social life of America's middle-middle, upper-middle, and upper classes," writes Herbert Wind. "At the clubhouse you lived with the people you wanted to associate with, played your bridge, drank your gin rickey, ate your guinea hen, danced your foxtrot, traded your tips on stocks, and gave your daughter away in marriage. Home was where you brought your dirty laundry — although the country club, in time, came to offer laundry service, valet service, a complete barber shop, a masseur, a dancing instructor. . . . Just name what you wanted and your country club had it. It was like some magnificent luxury liner that someone had forgotten to launch."

Life had never looked sweeter.

Chapter Seven

The Lean Years

The elation that had swept the club in the early and middle twenties — with the growing international fame of club member Bobby Jones and with the opening of two outstanding facilities and a second golf course in the same year — was not destined to last. "Right in the middle of all this the Great Depression of 1929 struck," writes Charles Elliott. "Banks closed. Stock market traders jumped out of tall buildings. U. S. business came virtually to a standstill. The country was in a fair way of going broke. In the midst of all this, AAC found itself with new properties, a decreasing membership, almost a million in debt, and hard put to even pay its managers and other personnel."

The club's ace in the hole for the depression years was not a fat savings account set aside for a rainy day, but something that would prove more valuable. It was the willpower of an individual — Scott Hudson. "The Club was run differently in those days," recalls Albert Happoldt, who served as manager of the downtown club under Hudson. "Clubs are run by committees now. In those days one man was law and order. Scott Hudson was the man."

Scott Hudson

Hudson had already established a record as an outstanding achiever before he became a member of the Athletic Club in 1911 at the age of 41. Born in the bluegrass country of Kentucky, the son of a mule trader, he became one of the most famous harness racers in the country. On July 25, 1902, he achieved a record that remains unmatched in harness racing by winning all four races scheduled for the day, each with a different horse. His total purse was $10,000.

By 1906 Hudson had disposed of most of his horse racing interests and moved to Atlanta with his wife to establish a livery stable on Marietta Street. There, he bought and sold horses and rented drays, wagons, and carriages.

Although he was middle-aged when he joined the Athletic Club and took up golf, he quickly became an outstanding golfer, on one occasion tucking his red hair into a baseball cap and shooting a 79 on the East Lake course to qualify for the Southern Amateur tournament. Yet, even as an avid golfer, Hudson, who became president in 1919, voted against building the number two course when it was proposed. An astute businessman, he was concerned that the club might be overextending itself.

Trying to Get a Grip

When Hudson's worst fears were realized in the crash of 1929, he did not hesitate. With ten years of the presidency behind him, he knew what was required and immediately became a full-time working president, without salary.

During this time William Burckel became general manager of both clubs, succeeding W. P. Felkner. (Burckel held the position of general manager for more than a decade.) The general manager's job involved supervising a staff of 35 people at Carnegie Way and 26 at East Lake. The year before the crash, Hudson had also hired Albert Happoldt, 23, then employed by the Biltmore Hotel, to replace George Richardson as manager of the Carnegie Way club. But it was Scott Hudson who, in fact, managed the two clubs. No one doubted it.

By assuming day-to-day management, Hudson reduced the expenses of the operations to some degree. But he knew he had to do more. He had to get a tight grip on every single expense.

One of the biggest expenses was food, so Hudson instructed Happoldt to buy in large quantities and at wholesale prices from the Atlanta Farmers' Market, then on Trinity Way. A strapping 6 feet tall and 150 pounds, Happoldt would rise at daylight to shop at the market (which closed at 7:00 a.m.) and return to the Carnegie Way club with the back seat and running boards of his car jammed with bags of vegetables and fruits. His wife Mary, who was his unofficial partner in running the club, went with him sometimes. "We bought supplies for two days," she remembers. "The club had a storage room, so we bought beans by the bushel, at 25 cents a bushel, and potatoes by the hundred. We used to go down there and get loaded up and get back to the club. Then we'd go upstairs and have breakfast and take a little rest."

Meanwhile Hudson, who lived on East Lake Drive, would have made his rounds at that club, personally assuming responsibility for the maintenance of the golf course. Under his supervision, J. O. Parker, a local farmer, kept the greens and fairways in condition using such homegrown supplies as the swamp cane (fashioned into brooms) to sweep the greens after they had been mowed. By 8:00 Hudson would be in his fifth-floor office at the Carnegie Way club, where he would pore over other ways to run the two-club and two-course organization on the dwindling amount of money at his disposal. The membership continued to drop away, one by one.

A story that has become part of the club's folklore illustrates Scott Hudson's dedication to reducing expenses during these years. One morning, the story goes, he had set out on the drive from East Lake to downtown when he spotted some familiar towels on his neighbor's clothesline. The towels seven of them, had the letters EAST LAKE printed on a red stripe through their center. Hudson went straight to his office and wrote a letter to his neighbor, advising him that, as of that moment, he was suspended from membership in the club. Membership privileges would be restored, he informed his neighbor, when the club's seven towels were.

As that story indicates, Hudson did not endear himself to every member during those years, but those who worked closely with him developed a deep affection for him. Happoldt tells this anecdote as an illustration of both sides of Scott Hudson:

> He raced horses and he used to have a private train that he carried his race horses in. He used to have grooms that looked after the horses, and they would go on the train and travel and feed them. One day he came into the dining room. One of his grooms had pancakes, and he was pouring pure maple syrup on them like it was water. Mr. Hudson said to him, "Ah, do you know how much that syrup costs?" And the groom says, "No, sir." "Well, it costs me $15 a gallon." The groom says "Yes, sir. And it's worth it, too!" He loved to tell that story.

Happoldt characterized Scott Hudson in this way:

SCOTT HUDSON, PRESIDENT 1918 - 1937
CHAIRMAN OF BOARD - 1937 TO 1946

E.A. THORNWELL, PRESIDENT 1943 TO 1946

HENRY C. HEINZ, PRESIDENT 1942-1943

ROBERT P. JONES, PRESIDENT 1937-1942

ATLANTA ATHLETIC CLUB PRESIDENTS — 1918-1944

Scott Hudson (upper left), president of the club from 1918 to 1937, became a full-time working manager during the depression years. Also pictured are three other club presidents.

"He liked to give the appearance of being a very gruff sort of person. Some people might say that he didn't have any heart. But he did. He had a heart of gold."

Dark Days

In the years 1929 to 1933, before Franklin D. Roosevelt became President of the United States and relieved the depression on the economy through his New Deal programs, Scott Hudson appeared to be fighting a losing battle for profits. The club had issued $100 certificates in 1926 (to furnish the Carnegie Way club), with the provision that they could be redeemed for cash at any time. As the Depression deepened, AAC members began to resign and cash in those certificates. Their counterparts in other cities were also resigning. "By 1931 the full impact of non-prosperity had struck home," writes Herbert Wind. "A number of the mammoth country clubs gave up after only a brief struggle. Expenses were as high as they had ever been, but club incomes had dropped as much as 65 percent."

"In those dark days the membership dropped from 1,250 to less than 500," writes Charles Elliott. "Those who could afford the nominal dues of $7 a month usually had pocketbooks too lean to allow for parties or entertainment or eating anywhere except at home, and the use of the Club dropped alarmingly." Arch Martin also remembers those days: "It was such a rough time. There was talk at one time during the Depression of the Capital City Club and the Athletic Club merging. That didn't work out. During the Depression so many people were out of jobs they just couldn't afford to belong to a club."

With the club Peggy Mitchell had called a magnificent luxury liner now sinking fast, no one wanted to assume the role of officer, so the same board remained in place. In 1930 the seven board members were Scott Hudson, Henry Heinz (treasurer), E. A. "Al" Thornwall, Bobby Jones, Alva Maxwell, A. A. Doonan, and William Burckel (secretary).

Hudson doggedly continued to operate the club, with the spectre of bankruptcy constantly at his shoulder. By 1932, the club had fallen into arrears on property taxes to the tune of $138,000.

On one memorable day bankruptcy appeared to be a certainty. The Prudential Insurance Company, which held the mortgage on the Carnegie Way club, paid Scott Hudson a visit. Hudson, the story is told, looked directly at his visitors and, without a word of apology, tossed them the keys. He had done everything he could, the gesture implied, and if they thought they could do better — well try it. They didn't. Not anxious to run a club, the company worked out new terms for repayment

Carnegie Way town club

45

and left the burden of management, once again, to Scott Hudson.

Bootstrap Survival

The solution did not come quickly, but it did come. The South, with its farming and textile economy, had not enjoyed the national prosperity of the 1920s, but neither did it suffer as long as the rest of the nation in the Depression.

The near-bankruptcy galvanized the club's membership into aggressive action. "This was a life-or-death matter," remembers Charles Elliott. "And the solution seemed to be more members. All remaining members got into the act as 'spark plugs,' with Lew Gordon as Spark Plug Chairman and Alva Maxwell leading the Glad-Hand Committee." Arch Martin adds, "We were letting members in without any initiation fees at all. We were glad to get them." Lew Gordon told the members they'd get two free tickets to dinner if they brought in a

new member. "I brought in a lot of members at that time," jokes Ralph Williams.

Gradually, says Elliott, "the club literally pulled itself up by its bootstraps, with every man a salesman. It was an extraordinary and superb job and the rolls went up again, slowly at first and with increasing vigor. Before the depression years wore themselves out, the membership strength was practically back to normal."

The board was increased from 7 to 11 members; Albert Happoldt became general manager of both clubs in 1941 (when George Bell resigned as manager of East Lake); and Scott Hudson, then in his seventies, was gradually able to give up the stresses of day-to-day management. But his influence would be felt by the staff for many years. "He was a stickler for members keeping their accounts up," says Clyde Mingledorff, who joined the club as auditor in 1943. "It was one of my responsibilities to make up an aging list of accounts receivable — to see who was 30 days behind, 60,

---

ANNUAL REPORT

of

MR. SCOTT HUDSON

President
Atlanta Athletic Club

1926-1927

Annual Report

FELLOW CLUB MEMBERS:

Since our last annual meeting both of our club buildings have been completed, furnished and put into operation. I do not think many of you realize the magnitude of this Organization. It is over a million and a half proposition, with 175 employees. For these two institutions to operate succesfully in so short a time is quite gratifying.

The cost of the land for the City building was $294,450.00, the cost of the building was $649,440.00. A total of $943,890.00. The cost of the furniture and equipment was $126,282.53. Every item pertaining to this building and equipment has been cleared and settled, except with the Flagler Company, the Contractors. We paid this company the total amount of their contract and for such extras as were approved by our architects and several weeks later, after we had taken possession, the Flagler Company filed claim of over $44,000.00, which our architects failed to approve, and which your Board thinks is unjust. This matter is now being arbitrated.

The East Lake Building cost $126,143.50, the furniture and fixtures $33,421.03. This practically represents the insurance collected. In other words: an even exchange for the old building and its contents.

Our interest bearing indebtedness is as follows: The Prudential Life Insurance Company $650,000.00. We are to retire this at the rate of 2½% each year. The Lynch Bonds of $175,005.00 we are to retire at the rate of $19,445.00 per year. The first issue fell due April 1, 1927 and was anticipated, discounted, and paid during February 1927. The first payment due the Prudential is June 12th. At this same date our semi-annual interest will be due to them. Both aggregate $34,125.00. I can see no reason why this should not be paid on time. If these annual payments are made, our interest decreases each year $2,251.90, and at the end of nine years the Lynch Mortgage Bonds should be retired: leaving only the Prudential loan, which should be reduced at that time to $503,750.00. Then your total interest and amortization charges will be less than $45,000.00 yearly, which is about half the present requirement and it is reduced at the rate of about $900.00 per year.

This club is well financed and the key to the plan was the Certificate of Deposit. This was not only a wonderful help to us when we needed

The annual report of 1927 warned members that the club was traveling on thin ice.

90, suspended, and what have you." He said, *"Don't let 'em get behind! If you do, it's part your fault!"*

In looking back on those years, the members are in agreement that the single force that saved the Athletic Club and allowed it to serve future generations was Scott Hudson. His passing on July 9, 1962, was observed with a formal printed tribute from the club as "the man who did more than any other to bring the Atlanta Athletic Club to its present stature." Says Arch Martin, "He was more than capable of running a downtown club and two golf courses at East Lake, which was quite an amazing thing, at no cost to the Athletic Club at all. You couldn't have hired anybody to take an interest in the club like that."

Gone Fishing

One of the pleasures that members recall the most during those depression years is fishing at East Lake. Charles Elliott, who was director of the Georgia Game and Fish Department at one time, describes the condition of the lake at the turn of the century:

Even before its acquisition by the Atlanta Athletic Club, East Lake was rated as good fishing waters and at least some of those who sought recreation far out in DeKalb County found it at the end of a long fishing pole. Early in its history there was no attempt at stocking or managing the lake for fish or fishing. After the dam was built to impound the flow from a dozen crystal springs, the lake received its population of fish by natural means, as have most newly created waters since the beginning of time. Herons and other wading birds, migrating from nearby waters at certain seasons of the year, brought in fish eggs on their legs to establish a number of local species such as bass, bream, catfish, and a variety of forage fish as prey for the game species.

Annual Report Atlanta Athletic Club

money but also in buying our furniture and equipment at a reasonable price for cash and besides it is the best collecting agency I have ever encountered. Not one dollar have we lost from members who have completed this payment. The losses charged off this year are for accounts made prior to this plan and the difference in this year's charge off and in former years proves its worth.

Your fixed charges include interest, retirement of bonds, amortization, taxes and insurance. These aggregate in round numbers one hundred thousand dollars annually. Your annual overhead estimated charges are:

Pay Rolls	$98,460.00	Light and Power	$13,200.00
Phones	4,500.00	Water	2,500.00
Laundry	8,400.00		

A total of $127,060.00. Add this to your fixed charges and you have $227,060.00 or $18,920.00 per month. You can readily see what is required of us to meet these payments together with our monthly purchases.

Our Membership is:

Resident	1297	Non-Resident	145
Juniors	70	Athletics	27
Specials	36	Judges	23
Army & Navy	7	Ladies	140

A total of 1746.

Fifteen months ago we had less than one thousand resident members. April 1, 1927 we have 1297. At least 500 of these have been elected in the past year, therefore our membership is 60% of our original members and 40% are new ones. This is a matter that must not be neglected. Our City Club was built for a 1,500 resident membership and it is up to you to produce them. This can only be handled by the membership at large, with this additional membership the going will be much easier.

Through the untiring efforts of Mr. Doonan we have been more than successful in athletics. We have many stars in Golf, Tennis, Basketball, swimming, etc. Bob Jones is the greatest asset any Club ever had. He gave us the opportunity and we have taken advantage of it.

To give you an idea of our growth; in 1919 your surplus was $155,048.16, in 1927 it is $444,331.02. An increase of $289,282.86 in

Annual Report Atlanta Athletic Club

eight years. We have not included in this amount the many thousand of dollars that were spent on East Lake Grounds and charged off to expense, nor have we taken advantage of any increase in land value. All of our land is carried at the same valuation today it was in 1919.

You will notice we have not charged off any depreciation on furniture and fixture at either club. Our plan has been in the past to hold this account as nearly stationary as possible. To do this any new equipment of any description is bought and paid for from the earnings at that time. Should we add these purchases, which are oft times quite heavy, to this furniture and fixture account it would be nearly impossible to charge off enough depreciation to hold it stationary. I think this the safest plan. A physical inventory of our furniture and equipment account would be greater than they are now carried on our books and it should be.

The clubs are now functioning much better than at any time since they opened. This is best illustrated by the increase in earnings in comparing July, 1926, the first month we operated, and March, 1927 the last month. A comparison of these two months gives March $3,902.46 advantage and practically every department is on the right side of the ledger.

Mr. Spring, our auditor, shows a profit for the year of $42,988.81. Now this looks good but when you deduct from this amount the annual retirement of bonds and amortization charges to the Prudential it leaves you only about eight thousand dollars. It is impossible for any organization of this magnitude to travel on any thinner ice. I do not think that it is possible to make very much improvements as to dollars and cents in the different departments and the only solution I can see for this matter is an increase in membership. Personally, I think we are over the rocks but I do not mean we can float without guiding, but with proper management, the continued support of the members, and an increased membership it should be much easier.

Mr. Richardson is to be congratulated upon his management. I have had the full support of the Board, the Committees, the Members and the Employees and without this it would have been impossible. To each I desire to express my appreciation.

SCOTT HUDSON, President.

April 19th, 1927.

Fishing at East Lake was a favorite diversion during the depression.

Bill (W.P.) Rocker proudly displays his catch at East Lake.

When the Athletic Club bought the East Lake property, golf was only a minor interest for most members. (Bobby Jones, whose family moved to East Lake in 1902, said the only licking he ever got from his dad was for playing hooky and fishing at East Lake.) They were just as likely to spend their hours fishing for bream, the fish the lake was noted for in those days. Even the geography of the lake was described in terms of where the bream beds lay. Swimmers knew that the competitive swimming course lay "between the bridge and the bream bed."

In 1920 the club decided to coax nature along a little by releasing 50,000 small fish into the lake and stashing brush along the banks to give them a place to hide from the bigger fish. They apparently needed the protection. The next year East Lake made the news when Ed Wight hauled in a 9½-pound bass. "He used an artificial minnow and landed the big fish in a minute and a half after hooking it," reported the *Atlanta Journal Magazine* of March 13, 1921. "The feat took place near No. 1 tee, opposite the clubhouse. The weight of the fish was verified in the post office by accurate scales." The article went on to describe one of the fish stories making the rounds at East Lake: "The ground keeper at East Lake says there's another fish in the lake — a bass — that must weigh at least 15 pounds. It has the habit of playing about in the early morning and of seeing how far it can jump out of the water. When it leaps back it sounds as though a whale had come to make East Lake its home."

With that, the bass fishing fever spread at East Lake and the number of fishers increased. By the time of the Depression, the lake was regularly managed to produce better fishing. Some 20,000 to 30,000 small fish, mostly fingerling bass and bream, were poured into the lake every year. The lake was drained periodically, to the complaints of many fishers, to eliminate the overbalance of certain species. And it was fertilized according to the recommendations of state and federal biologists. Daily fishing limits in the late thirties were 3 bass (not under 12 inches long) and 12 bream (not under 5 inches long). Later the limits would rise to 8 bass (not under 10 inches) and 35 bream (no size limit), with catfish added (7, not under 12 inches long).

The next report of a big bass catch came in 1940, when East Lake was being drained. The *Atlanta Journal Magazine* of October 27, 1940, again added to the big-fish lore, calling East Lake "the best lake in Georgia for bass":

> There are certain to be some mammoth fish [when the lake is drained]. Two years ago a huge carp was hemmed up in the weeds at the edge of the golf course, and killed with a niblick. The fish weighed a little over 30 pounds.
>
> Nobody knows how big the bass grow at East Lake. J. Dozier Lowndes, chairman of the lake and fish committee of the club, caught one that weighed 9 pounds and 2 ounces. . . . Members at East Lake may find that they have been harboring even bigger fish.
>
> On the bottom should be some catfish that would scare Jonah. You know fish can grow pretty big in the length of time East Lake has been in existence.

The article went on to describe why East Lake had developed its reputation for good fishing:

> In the first place, fingerlings brought in for restocking get the best break ever offered to young bass. These small fry are turned loose in the two rearing pools, where they are fed a good growing diet. And no fish bigger than themselves are admitted to the pools, so every

new bass has a chance to grow up. Five thousand fingerlings mean 5,000 nice young bass to be driven out into the lake a few months later.

> The lake covers 43 acres, which is just the right size any way you look at it. The water is 18 feet deep in the middle, which gives the big fellows an icy bath on the bottom throughout the summer, and there are plenty of warm shallows around the edges for the small fry.
>
> Water for the lake comes from numerous springs on the bottom. It is always cold when it seeps out of the ground, just right for game fish. There are drainage ditches all around the lake to keep muddy surface water from getting in.

In that environment the fish grew, and so did the fish stories.

In 1948 Walter N. Pendleton, Jr., topped earlier records and thrilled every fishing member by hooking a monster of a large mouth bass (a 10-pound, 4-ounce lunker, 26 inches long) off one of the piers. By this time Bobby Jones, now disabled from syringomyelia, had returned to the pleasure of his childhood days and could often be seen fishing at East Lake. "When he was still playing golf he thought fishermen were a bunch of stupid people," bantered Bill Street. "But after he couldn't play golf and started fishing, he thought people who played golf were kind of stupid."

Eventually East Lake turned over the management of the lake to the Game and Fish Commission, which provided management, draining, seining, and restocking of the lake on a scientific basis.

Corn Liquor

Another favorite diversion for letting off steam during the depression years was devising ways to get around the national prohibition laws that were in effect from 1920 to 1933.

Happoldt remembers receiving deliveries of moonshine corn whiskey from north Georgia at the Carnegie Way club. "They delivered it in the front door of the club kind of late at night — about 10:00. A policeman would always be there — timed it real well. And he would say, 'Hap, what's that thing they're bringing into the club?' I would say, 'It ain't none of your business.' He would say, 'I know what you're talking about and I'll stay out of it.' "

"It came in charred kegs," remembers Ralph Williams. "That was the only way they could make it where you could swallow it, it tasted so bad. You would mix it with grapefruit juice to kill the taste. Sometimes you didn't know where it came from, so you would test it. You would pour a little bit out and strike a match to it. If there was a blue flame, you knew it wasn't alcohol . . . but I never knew anyone who turned it down." According to Arch Martin, corn whiskey that had been stored in a charred keg for a year "was as good as your 8-year liquor. We kept our liquor in our lockers out at East Lake — two 5-pound kegs would fit into one locker."

A favorite employee during this period was Al Dandridge, who had been with the club as locker room attendant since 1904. At Carnegie Way during the late 1920s, he assumed control of the locker-room liquor commerce, just as he had at the Auburn Avenue club. For many members, the friendliness, wit, and philosophies of Dandridge were as important to their good cheer as was the corn whiskey, and they delighted in telling stories about him and the good times at both clubs.

One of the best-known stories, according to Charles Elliott, comes from the early and middle 1920s, when Internal Revenue Service agents waged an all-out campaign against the private clubs, hoping both to dry up the supply of illegal whiskey and to make an example of influential men in the community. The old AAC on Auburn Avenue was one of the clubs under constant surveillance by IRS agents. Two of these agents made friends with Al Dandridge, who knew them only as guests and friends of a newer club member.

After exercise and showers one day in the gym, the two agents sat down to pass the time of day with Dandridge in the locker room. Bantering along with some irrelevant questions, one of the men finally asked,

"Do you have much drinking in the locker room?"

Dandridge rolled his eyes. "Lordy, yes!"

The agents exchanged glances. "Well, I guess that's natural," the other said, matter-of-factly.

"Who are some of the fellows who have a drink here?"

Dandridge obligingly reeled off the names of many top-ranking members, including some on the board of directors.

"Do you serve them?"

"Yessir, I shore do."

Smelling pay dirt, the agent asked, "What do you serve mostly?"

Dandridge puckered his brow. "Well, let's see now. Mr. Jones, when he gets out of his cold shower, always likes a pot of hot tea, with lemon but no sugar. Now Mr. Smith, he don't take nothing like that atall, but I have to get him a glass of buttermilk from the kitchen. Mr. Woodruff, now he won't drink nothing but Coca-Cola — you know, he's the Coca-Cola man — and then there's . . ."

"Aw, hell," interrupted the agent. "Thanks, anyway, Al. You're a real gentleman, and a smart one. Guess we'll have to get our information from some other source."

(Al Dandridge died in 1940, after 36 years with the Athletic Club.)

By 1933 prohibition was over and so was the worst of the Depression. Atlanta's growth had continued through the lean years, reaching a level of 270,366 in 1930, and the city was beginning to emerge as the leader among Southern cities. Long a transportation center, Atlanta stepped into a new age in 1930, when both Delta and Eastern Airlines started scheduled passenger service from Hartsfield Airport.

Both the city and the Athletic Club would again experience rapid growth in the future. But, sobered by the harsh realities of the Depression, neither would quickly regain the unqualified confidence of earlier years. The grim experience of the lean years would affect the club's decisions for decades to come.

Chapter Eight

Outstanding Golfers of Mid-Century

It is one of the ironies of the history of the Athletic Club — and a mark of its strength — that in 1930, at the very time when the future of the club came into question, Bobby Jones led it to its greatest victory by winning the Grand Slam in golf. From that glorious moment on, the Depression notwithstanding, the world spotlight was on the Athletic Club. And the club came through. For the next three decades the club produced one outstanding golfer after another. One of the most prominent was Charles R. Yates.

Charlie Yates

"One afternoon we were sitting up at the old 19th hole that used to overlook the 9th green,"

Charlie Yates was known as much for his personality as for his championship golf.

Bobby Jones told Charles Elliott, "and this youngster was playing and came along. He put his second

shot over the lake, about 75 yards short of the green and pitched up about three or four feet from the hole. He had a beautiful swing, and at the table where we were sitting someone said, 'That kid swings like a champ. Isn't it a shame that since his father and mother are so small, he'll really never grow up big enough to play championship golf.' "

The "kid" they were talking about was Charlie Yates, who would top 6 feet and bring home championships in the National Collegiate, Western Amateur, and British Amateur tournaments, not to mention a Walker Cup team championship.

Yates was conscious of Bobby Jones long before he earned the notice of the golfing king in return. By the time Yates started slipping over the East Lake fence from his grandfather's house across the street from the fourth tee, Jones (11 years his senior) already carried the aura of a champion. Young Charlie and his friends (including Bill Street) trailed along behind the champ, just as Jones had tagged along after Stewart Maiden. "Sometimes he would take us into the clubhouse and buy us that great delight of Atlanta called Coca-Cola, or he would give us some golf balls," remembers Yates. "On occasion, when we were still under 10, he would even play a few holes with us."

Young Charlie empathized strongly with his hero, crushed by his losses and elated by his victories. "I remember one time when he had lost and had been runner-up, as he was on a number of occasions. I went up to him when he got back to the club and congratulated him on how well he played and told him how sorry I was that he had lost," says Yates. "He said, 'Well, Charlie, don't worry about it, boy. After all, a fellow never knows who his friends are until he has lost. When everything isn't going right, you can tell who's with you.' " When Bobby Jones broke his chain of losses by winning the U.S. Open in 1923, Yates, 10, who

As a boy, Charlie Yates trailed along behind Bobby Jones, just as Jones had followed Stewart Maiden.

Harold Sargent, East Lake and Atlanta Athletic Club golf pro from 1926 to 1979, was founder of the city's Junior Golf program.

had heard it on the radio, barrelled out of his grandfather's house and tore over to the course, yelling out the news to every golfer in sight.

By this time Yates had taken to golf pretty strongly himself, hopping on the streetcar to East Lake every day after school to play. When his younger sister began to outswim him a couple of years later, his commitment to golf was confirmed. By the time he entered Georgia Tech, Yates was an accomplished golfer, even in the stellar company of Tech's golf team, which included Tommy Barnes, Berrien Moore, Scott Hudson, Jr., and Bill Street, among others. With so many East Lake members on the team and with their practices held at the East Lake course, the Tech team seemed to be an extension of the Athletic Club.

The Sargents

It was no coincidence that this group of outstanding athletes developed at a time when a second family of golf pros were affiliated with East Lake — the Sargents. George Sargent, born in Epsom Downs, England, was the first of the family to serve as East Lake's pro, and he came to the club from a strong professional career as a golfer. He had won the U.S. Open in 1909, setting the record for the all-time low score, and the Canadian Open in 1912, again with a record score. He had then served as pro at some of the country's best-known clubs, including Chevy Chase in Washington, D.C. (where he instructed President Taft), Interlachen in Minnesota (where Bobby Jones won the U.S. Open in 1930), and Scioto in Columbus, Ohio (where Jones won the 1926 U.S. Open).

In 1932 George Sargent came to East Lake, following behind Frank Ball, Billy Watson, and Charlie Gray. (Stewart Maiden had left AAC to open an indoor golf school in the Grand Central Building in New York. He would later return to Atlanta as pro for the Peachtree Golf Club.) Hugh Wilson, who was then an East Lake golfer, remembers a technique Sargent brought with him. "He attempted to teach us the Varden swing, from Harry Varden of England. Instead of starting the golf swing as most people would, as a one-piece swing, it was started with loose hands. They called it the Varden Drag. The hands moved and the club head dragged behind and supposedly that would help you make a better turn from the ball." Wilson found it hopeless, but admits, "It worked with Harry Varden. And George Sargent won the U.S. Open using it in 1909."

George's son Harold, who assisted his father, remembers that the crafting of clubs was still a part of the pro's job in the early thirties. "One Monday in 1932 we put in 19 hickory shafts. The club was

Jack Sargent, flanked by his brother Harold, holds a portrait of his father George. The three served respectively as golf pros for the club from 1932 to 1985.

a great club-throwing club. They got this from Bob Jones. I guess they just thought it was the thing to do." One of the reasons George Sargent was able to accommodate the demand for club-making was a good-natured employee in the golf shop remembered simply as Woodrow. He kept up with cleaning, maintenance, and repair of the clubs and won a place in the affection of members.

George Sargent remained at the Athletic Club until his retirement in 1947, serving as president of the PGA from 1920 to 1926. His son Harold then took over the reins. Although he was never the serious professional contender on the golf circuit his father had been, he continued the tradition of leadership in the golfing community, serving as president of the PGA in 1958, 1959, and 1960. In Atlanta, he was one of those who founded the city's Junior Golf program, coaching the first junior team to participate in the Havalanta sports competition between Atlanta and Havana, Cuba. Harold would, in turn, be succeeded by his brother Jack Sargent in 1979, after 47 years with AAC.

The Sargents, like the Maidens in the early part of the century, carried on a tradition of fine golf instruction at East Lake and conveyed high respect for the history of the sport and the club's place in that history. In doing so, they nurtured the outstanding golfers of mid-century, athletes who would take their places in golfing history.

Yates Stands Tall

Under the tutelage of George Sargent and Hubert F. Dennison, coach of the Tech golf team, Charlie Yates' devotion to golf began to pay off. In 1935, at the age of 22, he became U.S. Intercollegiate Champion, and the next year he won the Western Amateur championship.

The next two years brought no big wins for Yates. They were dues-paying years as he followed the golf circuit. In 1937 he was joined by a younger teammate at Tech, Thomas W. Barnes, who had attracted the city's attention by winning both the Atlanta Open and the Atlanta Amateur

53

Talented women golfers also developed at East Lake.

that year. (Although Barnes was an AAC member as well, he played as a representative of Druid Hills Golf Club.) Barnes, Yates, and sportswriter O. B. Keeler made the tour together that year, passing through Chicago, Vancouver, and Seattle en route to the U.S. Amateur championship in Portland and the Western Amateur in Los Angeles. Keeler later wrote about the trip under the headline, "Ten Nights in a Pullman."

The trip produced no crowns for the Tech teammates, but it was an imminently successful warm-up. In 1938 Barnes won the Southern Intercollegiate Championship. And Yates gave Atlantans a thrill they had not felt since Bobby Jones: he won the British Amateur in Troon, Scotland, at the age of 25.

Ralph McGill, longtime editor of *The Atlanta Constitution,* attended the match and described his thoughts at the time:

> Trudging along behind Charlie Yates as he marched through wind and rain and sun to win the British amateur golf championship at Troon, I found myself thinking of East Lake and its members.
>
> The old tradition had come alive again, and here, after a lapse of eight years, was another golfer from East Lake bringing terror and dark days to British golf. East Lake was on the march, and I hoped the members appreciate what it means to be a member of the East Lake club, a club known wherever golf is played. Thousands were asking how one club could produce so many fine golfers, and two British amateur champions within so short a span.
>
> I knew how the locker room faithfuls, and the caddies and attendants, and fine George Sargent were suffering as the field grew smaller and smaller. But Yates remained at the end of each day, until at last the day came when he and East Lake were left to fight a lone battle for America.
>
> As long as golf is a subject of conversation, they will tell of that Friday when his eagle 'two' shook Cyril Tolley, and of his really magnificent comeback to catch Hector Thompson at the eighteenth and beat him at the nineteenth with as bold and fine a putt as golf has seen. Ten thousand men and women cheered him when the putt dropped and he looked up, a finalist.
>
> The next day he won the championship from a big Irishman. East Lake and Atlanta had done it again.

McGill's words thrilled AAC members, who had been hoping against the odds for another really big winner.

The British immediately took a liking to this second Atlanta to win the British Amateur crown. They still had a fondness for that first American 6-footer, whose modesty and politeness had captured their hearts. This second tall and handsome American impressed them with the strength and boldness of his swing. "Yates . . . hit the ball wonderfully well in winning the British Amateur," writes Herbert Wind. "Everything was coming into his strenuous swing at the right time, and several Scots who had witnessed Charley's impressive march were almost convinced that what was holding back British golfers was that they didn't dip their knees as Yates did when he hurled his right side viciously into his shots. The Scots cottoned on to Yates as soon as they heard he was a fellow-townsman of Bobby Jones', and Charley's forcing golf and rich sense of humor made him the most popular man in Scotland."

Charlie Yates became one of the legends of East Lake, not only for his winning golf, but also for his winning personality; he was and is known as one of the best storytellers of the club, always downplaying his own achievements. He considered himself only one among many good golfers at East Lake. "I have often thought how well I played sometimes in tournaments and got the daylights beaten out of me," he remarked to acquaintances some years later.

Johnny Comes Marching Home

World War II changed the everyday lives of Americans in many ways. But the end result for East Lake was that it increased the popularity of golf.

While the war was in progress, life at East Lake continued much the same for most members, with minor inconveniences. "Three-quarters of the clubs in the United States remained open throughout the war," writes Herbert Wind. "Few of them took up the U.S.G.A.'s suggestion that part of their roughs be turned into victory gardens, and the members of the Wykagyl Golf Club were almost alone in ploughing up their first two holes and allotting a plot to be worked by each of the fifty-five member families. . . . Courses could not be maintained as they had been in peacetime, for power mowers had broken down and the strongbodied minions of the greenkeeper were in uniform, but the home-front golfer, for all of his handicaps, played just about as well as he had in 1941 except when members of his draft board were in the foursome immediately in front or behind him." East Lake was

A skillful East Lake foursome checks their golf scores. L — R: Bob Ingram, Tommy Barnes, Bob Jones, Henry Lindner — July 16, 1948.

one of those clubs that sponsored a victory garden.

Those who were at war were also playing more than a little golf. Most military bases provided a golf course and many men took up the sport for the first time, bringing their enthusiasm for golf back home with them when they returned.

Tommy Barnes was among the Atlantans who returned from the war better golfers than when they left. In 1946 he won the Southeastern Open and in 1947 captured the South's top crown, the Southern Amateur, which he won again in 1949.

Master Caddy Master

The end of the war also brought East Lake an employee who would become one of its most valued — James Robert Brett. Before the war, Brett had served for 12 years as caddy master at Nassau Country Club, near Glen Cove on Long Island. But when he returned after the war in 1945, he found his old job taken by a man with a large family and decided not to ask for it back. Instead he advertised for a position as caddy master in *Golfdom Magazine* and received an offer from East Lake.

With the increase in golfing interest, East Lake badly needed his skills. "Before the Brett era, there was always confusion around the golf shop door," remembers Charles Elliott, "with each swinger trying to get his favorite caddy and the caddies making attempts to team up with the golfer who gave out with the largest tip." Jim Brett soon set the system to rights and made it understood that every golfer would get the same treatment from him. With some 200 golfers playing on Sundays during the late 1940s, it was a necessary rule.

The story is told that Bobby Jones, waiting to tee off one day, decided to go back inside the clubhouse for a snack. When he came back he'd missed his tee time and was advised by Brett, "You are now eighth in line, Mr. Jones." Charles Ponder remembers, "If you wanted to get scheduled he'd say, 'Is everybody in the foursome here?' "

Working with a roster that grew to include 150 caddies, Brett trained, disciplined, and mothered his team to provide the polite service he expected. "You didn't have to rent a cart," marvels Arch Martin in remembering those days. "You had a caddy who carried your bags for probably fifty cents — for 18 holes."

The members soon learned to value Jim Brett's way of doing business and, over the course of some 40 years, came to regard him as one of the club's major assets. "He had only two things on his mind," says Ponder, "golf at the Athletic Club and the stock market." On golf, Jim Brett became a walking encyclopedia. Gifted with a photographic memory, he could reel off the scores of every major tournament and describe the background of almost any player of the last quarter-century. His stock market interest began with a tip from an AAC member. Brett eventually accumulated such a portfolio that his accountant advised him to retire — his job was costing him money. He ignored the advice, but when members learned of it they gave him the nickname "Dow Jones."

In 1961 the club honored him with a tribute that described exactly how he handled the caddy operation:

When you are golfward bound and walk through the door into the golf shop, you meet Jimmy Brett, give him the names in your foursome, or tell him how many players you need to make your game. You eat your lunch, change your clothes and complete whatever other activities are prelude to your play. In the meantime, if you need players to complete your foursome, the caddy master, who knows just about every one of the three or four hundred regular players, their handicaps and temperaments, and who they like or do not like to play with, is sorting out golfers to find suitable players to fill out your game. If a qualified prospect comes along, Jimmy handles the contacts between him and the potential foursome in such a manner that almost without exception, any player or group of players may accept or turn down a game without embarrassment of any kind. And that, fellow hackers, is the essence of diplomacy!

Your game is made. When you appear again at the golf shop door, your clubs have been set out, your caddy is waiting, and the odds are exceedingly large that he'll be a good caddy. We don't have many of the other kind, which is another tribute to the efficiency of this particular operation.

Brett remained with the Athletic Club for 37 years. When he died suddenly of pneumonia on March 29, 1982, Jim Petzing (general manager at the time) said, in a formal tribute, "Golf and the Atlanta Athletic Club have lost one of their family."

It was during Brett's era with AAC that another outstanding golfer developed at the club: Charles W. Harrison. In 1952, at the age of 20 he won the city championship and defended the title for the next two years. Then in 1955 Harrison won the Southern Amateur title in Linville, North Carolina, rallying from a four-stroke deficit to defeat Billy Joe Patton.

His trophy for the tournament carried unusual significance, as the *Club Times* of October 15 that year pointed out: "An interesting sidelight to Charlie Harrison's winning this trophy springs from the fact that it is known as the George W. Adair

trophy and was presented by Mr. Adair, president of the AAC from 1905 to 1911. He is founder of the Adair Realty & Loan Company, where Charlie Harrison is now employed as a junior executive and is associated with Jack Adair, son of the trophy's donor."

Harrison had become part of a tradition made possible by George Adair. Adair had believed Atlanta was ready for the new sport of golf when he encouraged the Athletic Club to start a country club back in 1904. In proving him right, Alexa Stirling and Bobby Jones had started a tradition of national and international excellence, and it had been upheld by Watts Gunn, Charlie Yates, Tommy Barnes, and now Charlie Harrison, among male golfers. It had also been upheld by talented female golfers.

Great Women Golfers

Although the Athletic Club had been organized as a men's club, women took an active role in golfing from the time the sport was introduced at East Lake. Alexa Stirling was the club's first great golfer at East Lake, holding the U.S. Women's Amateur title from 1916 through 1920. (No tournaments were held in 1917 and 1918.) Margaret Maddox continued the tradition by winning the Southern Women's tournament in 1929. And by mid-century the club was again contributing to the making of national women's champions — honorary mem-

Charlie Harrison upheld the East Lake tradition of national excellence.

Golfers and fans check the day's tournament scores.

Competition was keen at the East Lake course, site of many women's tournaments.

Although the Athletic Club was organized as a men's club, women took an active role in golfing from the time the sport was introduced at East Lake.

bers Louise Suggs and Dorothy Kirby. Both women officially played for other clubs but credited much of their skill to the influence of East Lake's "number one course" and the support of East Lake golfers.

Dot Kirby, who was introduced to golf on a "Tom Thumb" putting course next to her family's apartment on Piedmont Avenue in Atlanta, was only 13 in 1933 when she defeated Margaret Maddox, two up, to win the state women's championship played at East Lake. Kirby says of Maddox, "She was so good. She was the first person I had played who had a name and a reputation." After her win, *Collier's* ran a cover photo of Dot Kirby and Bobby Jones. Four years later, at 17, Kirby won the Women's Southern, also played at East Lake defeating Estelle Lawson Page, who went on to win the U.S. Women's title the same year.

In the 1940s Louise Suggs, three years younger (and the daughter of Atlanta Crackers pitcher Johnny Suggs), eclipsed her fellow Atlantan. Described by Herbert Wind as "a supple youngster who could develop such clubhead velocity that she was rightfully termed the Ben Hogan of women's golf," she won the state title in 1940 (at 17), the Southern title in 1941, the Women's North-South and Women's Titleholders in 1942, and the Western Open and Western Amateur in 1947. In 1948 Louise Suggs became the first golfer to win the women's Grand Slam by taking all four major U.S. titles: the U.S. Women's National, the Women's Southern, the Women's Western Open, and the Women's Western Amateur.

Suggs' closest competitor was Dot Kirby, who was runner-up in three of the four tournaments. And Kirby, who loved competitive play, was not about to give up on the national title. In September 1950 she was Atlanta's major contender when the U.S. Women's Amateur was held in Atlanta. Mattie (Mrs. W. D.) Tumlin had arranged for the tournament to be played at East Lake, and on the eve of the match, O. B. Keeler speculated on Kirby's prospects in the September 10 *Atlanta Constitution Magazine:*

> This is the third time the Women's National has been played south of what the Yankees call the Smith & Wesson Line, in 1928 at Hot Springs, Va., and in 1937 at the Memphis Country Club, where Mrs. Julius A. Page, the erstwhile Estelle Lawson, of Chapel Hill, N.C., won it, after being defeated a few weeks earlier at East Lake by Dorothy Kirby in the Women's Southern. Estelle, incidentally, was the first Southern entry to win the National since Atlanta's and East Lake's Alexa Stirling's third victory in succession, away back in 1920....

As for the performance around this truly distinguished golf course, as lately developed under the smooth regime of the distinguished veteran professional, George Sargent, U.S. champion in 1909, and Hal Sargent, his son and successor, predictions at this stage are in the always charming phase of guessing. As stated, the defending champion is in the field, — and Mrs. Porter has become a mother since winning at Merion last year, something of a record, and she has been playing well for a decade as Dorothy Germain, when she didn't have so much housework on her chest. . . .

Atlanta's got a prime number in there, of course. Dorothy Kirby, who won the Georgia State at the age of 13 — at East Lake — and the Southern at 17. Dorothy Kirby, runner-up to Betty Jameson in the National at Wee Burn in 1939, and to Louise Suggs in 1947 at Franklin Hills, in the greatest match the ladies have ever played in the U.S.G.A. championship, a member of the Curtis Cup in 1948 and 1950, a national figure for more than a decade. Dorothy

Kirby will be in there pitching and putting, over a home town layout, which she knows fairly well, you might say. Who knows? It might be her turn.

It wasn't. Beverly Hanson took home the prize.

It was then that a fellow East Lake golfer, Bobby Jones, stepped in. "I always had a problem with 'quickhooking' the ball off the tee in tournaments," says Kirby. "I lost a lot of matches that way. One day Bob called me and said, 'I think I can help you with that.' He gave me lesson after lesson to get me out of that, sitting in a chair because by that time he couldn't walk much." Jones' tutoring worked. In 1951, competing at the Town and Country Club course in St. Paul, Minnesota, Kirby brought home the national championship, becoming the second Atlantan to win the title within five years and the third in history.

While Kirby was setting the national pace for Atlanta, several women golfers at East Lake were consistently winning titles at home. Among them were Mrs. Harold Denson, Mrs. Larry Martin, Mrs.

Gladys Denson (with trophy) was a frequent winner at East Lake golf tournaments. Others pictures are front row, L — R: Pearl Prather, Nickie Barches, Gladys Denson, Thelma Martin, Katherine Senkheil. Back Row: Eileen Gunnell,

Connie Wilson, Mildred Stone, Ann Warner, Helen DeWies, Jo Donohue, Louise Keely, Margaret Deiters, Jan Guler, Alice Boykin, Marie Bellinger, Mary Sargent, Virginia Nosworthy.

Mrs. Fred Bellinger and Mrs. Fred Donohue, President of East Lake Women's Golf Assocation, consistently won golf tournaments at East Lake.

It was one of those times when golfing excellence begat golfing excellence and East Lake was fortunate it had an Alexa Stirling and a Bobby Jones to set the tradition.

Fred Bellinger, and Mrs. Fred Donohue, with Joyce Denson attracting notice in junior girls play. In a very unusual tournament, Joyce Denson, 16, competed against her mother, Mrs. Harold Denson, in the Atlanta Women's Golf Championship finals on September 13, 1957. Joyce won over her mother 3-2 in the final.

Ryder Cup at East Lake

A second major tournament — the British-American Ryder Cup Match — was scheduled at East Lake's number one course for October 1963 and this time the popular course got a three-year face-lift. The most fundamental change was converting the greens to bent grass. Eugene Brooks, chairman of the East Lake committee, and Jim Fischer, sitting in the early mornings on the terrace overlooking the course, mulled over the idea of a year-round grass. Like most Southern courses the greens were sodded in bermuda, which served as the summer cover, and in the winter rye grass was planted over the bermuda. "That bermuda — with those runners — was like putting on grape vines," remembers Tommy Barnes. "That was one of the big disadvantages I had when we played in national tournaments on fast bent grass. It made a tremendous difference in putting."

With bent grass now improved enough to survive Atlanta's hot summers, Fischer and Brooks fially decided that the time had come to convert. They recruited Mel Warnecke as course superintendent in 1958 (from the Country Club of Indianapolis) and gave him the task of testing bent grass on East Lake's course. After it proved stable on the ninth and eighteenth greens, the remaining greens were planted in bent grass.

Under the direction of course architect George Cobb, Warnecke rebuilt a number of the holes in the process. The greens were enlarged to championship size, underlaid with drainage tile and crushed stone, covered with soil and topsoil, and resodded, with built-in sprinkler systems. Bunkers were also enlarged and 30 were added.

The tournament, played over the beautiful redesigned course, drew such top professionals as Arnold Palmer, Gary Player, Jay Hebert, Tony Lema, Doug Ford, George Beyer, Bo Wininger, Bob Goalby, Bob Rosburg, Billy Casper, Art Wall, Jr., and Gay Brewer, Jr. Crowds ranged from 7,500 to 12,000. And the American team, led by Arnold Palmer, was victorious, winning handily 23 to 9.

East Lake had held her own and then some in the world spotlight that had shone on the club since Charlie Yates' victory in 1938. More and more Atlantans, male and female, had taken to the courses. Under the tutelage of the Sargents, many of them had made their mark in golf. Others had not, but they had been good athletes, nonetheless, and formed a knowledgeable and appreciative gallery for those who became stars. As sportswriter Morgan Blake had observed in the December 1925 *City Builder*, "Atlanta is the leader in sports not only because of the outstanding athletic stars that live here, but also because of the fact that the city boasts thousands and thousands of the finest sportsmen and sportswomen in the land. These laymen in athletics may not enter activity [sic] into the various games, but they are vitally interested in them, do a powerful lot of looking on, and back them to the limit." That camaraderie was much in evidence at East Lake. Years later, Tommy Barnes commented, "We'd have a state amateur and there'd be 3,000 people in the galleries. I've never seen that kind of spirit in any other club."

It was one of those times when golfing excellence begat golfing excellence, and East Lake was fortunate it had an Alexa Stirling and a Bobby Jones to set the tradition. Wherever Southern or national tournaments were played during the early and middle part of the century, AAC could be counted on to furnish, at least, an outstanding competitor. And, often, a champion.

Chapter Nine

The Growth Years

The recovery from the Depression came gradually for the Atlanta Athletic Club, but as hard times began to loosen their grip on the country, the club's growth picked up. From a low of 500 in 1932, membership climbed back to 1,000 in 1936, and in 1945 (with the economy stimulated by World War II) it reached an all-time high of 3,300. Bobby Jones' fame was a major drawing card.

The Aura of Bobby Jones

Somewhat to Jones' dismay, he had become a legend in his own time. Charlie Yates likes to tell the story of when Jones and a friend attended the national championship in 1937 in Portland, Oregon. "He was watching the final match between Johnny Goodman and Ray Billows. They were having a good match, but Ray always looked like he was going to get beaten because Johnny was playing a lot more consistent. On the twelfth hole, Ray pulled his drive by the great big, bushy tree, and he was about 160 yards from the green. Johnny hit a beautiful drive down the fairway and Bob says, 'Let's go up there and watch Ray play this shot — I want to see how he plays it.' They stood on this little mount right behind. Just before Ray made his shot a couple of strangers came up and joined them on the mound. Ray hit the most magnificent shot you ever saw. It went around that tree and hooked like it had eyes and got on the green about six feet away from the hole. There was a tremendous applause, and when it died down Bob said to his friend, 'That's the greatest golf shot I ever saw in my life. I don't think anybody else playing golf could play that just like Billows did.' This stranger said, 'Say, Mister, you don't know what in the hell you're talking about. Bobby Jones could play that shot much better than Billows just did.' Bob looked him in the eye and said, 'Well, I don't believe he could.' That fellow stuck his jaw out like he was going to have a fit and said, 'Say, Mister, did you ever see that son

of a bitch play?' Bob walked off. The fella never knew who he called an SOB."

Robert W. Woodruff, AAC member and president of the Coca-Cola Company at that time, told a similar story before his death in 1985. Woodruff was playing golf at the famous St. Andrews course when, on the fifth hole (a long par 5), he hit three nice shots to the green. Along with him was one of the longtime professional Scottish caddies. They walked up to the green, but instead of complimenting the shot, the caddy sniffed, "When I caddied for Bobby Jones, he was here in two." Woodruff, planning to have a bit of fun, said placidly, "Who's Bobby Jones?" The Scot stood stunned for a full minute, staring down the Coca-Cola magnate, then, without a word, slipped the golf bag off his shoulder, turned on his heel and walked back to the clubhouse. "And he didn't come back," Woodruff would later chuckle as he recounted the story.

That kind of hero worship from strangers brought many visitors to East Lake and many of those became club members. But if Bobby Jones was the primary source of the club's fame, his father, Robert Purmedus Jones, affectionately known as "Colonel Bob," was its spiritual leader. (Bobby was named for his grandfather.)

Colonel Bob

Colonel Bob was one of the most colorful personalities in the club's history, and for many he is a symbol of the good times members spent together during the growth years of the thirties and forties. An excellent athlete in his own right, he had once signed a contract to play professional baseball with the Brooklyn Club of the old National League, only to have his father forbid such foolishness. But the Colonel (a common title for respected attorneys of the time) was determined to carry a little "foolishness" into his law practice and social life. He was apt to break into "Old Man River" or "Home on the Range" in the locker room at East Lake (or even in the drawing room of his good friend Robert Woodruff), and he was sure to start off board meetings with a joke during the years when he was president (1937 to 1942). During one meeting a member supposedly asked, "Well, what is a club, anyway?" Without missing a lick, the Colonel shot back, "A club is a group of fellows who band themselves together to build and enjoy facilities that no one of the group could do alone, with the express privilege of paying more money for it."

Through the force of his personality, the Colonel became the center of countless stories, most of them about his golf or his spicy vocabulary. He had a reputation for a terrible golf swing, except on the practice tee. One day at the clubhouse he reportedly showed his swing to his son Bobby and asked, "Son, what's the matter with that swing?" "Nothing." his son replied. "Why don't you use it sometime?"

A favorite story about the Colonel's cussing involved a tournament between East Lake and another club in a town outside Atlanta. Some of the members learned that the other club had a member with every bit as strong a reputation for profanity as the Colonel. So the tournament committee arranged for the two men to play in the same foursome, telling each the same story — that he was playing against a preacher and, as a courtesy, must watch his language.

"Everyone who was in on the joke declared that it was probably the most hilarious round of golf ever played," recounts Charles Elliott. "When one of the contestants missed a shot — which was often — instead of going into his usual verbal barrage . . . he would turn red in the face, controlling his temper with obvious effort. This went on for fourteen holes, with the other members of the foursome and the gallery scarcely able to contain their own hilarity.

"On the 15th hole, the Colonel's opponent missed a short putt. As he stepped over to pick up his ball on the edge of the cup, he said under his breath, 'goddamnedsonofabitch!' The foursome froze for an instant and Colonel Bob, only a step away, reached over and caught the man by the arm.

" 'What did you say?' he asked.

" 'Why it was nothing — nothing,' the golfer stammered.

" 'What did you *say*?' he demanded.

"His opponent faced him, red to the tips of his ears. 'Look, preacher,' he apologized, 'I couldn't help it. It just slipped out. I'm sorry.'

" 'Preacher!' Colonel Bob roared. 'Who's a preacher?'

" 'They told me you were,' the man mumbled, and the two stared at one another, the light beginning to dawn.

"Those who followed the match later declared that the air was blue from that point on to the clubhouse."

The Colonel was often seen playing in a foursome with his son Bobby, Dick Garlington, and Robert Woodruff. Stories also grew up around each of these golfers. Bill Street told this story on Robert Woodruff, who, according to Street, usually arrived at the clubhouse with two cars — one for himself and one for his clubs. "He had a reputation of kind of fudging a little bit. One day he was playing on number 12 and he knocked his ball out in the woods. We all had to hunt it. One of the men in the foursome said, 'I'm going to fix him up this time.' He found the ball and picked it up. We walked on down the fairway, and a few minutes later a ball whizzed by our heads and Mr. Woodruff said, 'Look at this. I found my ball back there.' This fellow said, 'How did you find it? I've got it in my pocket!' "

Being caught in such indiscretions apparently never harmed Robert Woodruff's friendships. "He never took golf seriously," explains J. W. Jones, Woodruff's personal secretary for many years and, ultimately, corporate secretary. "If he missed a putt, he would pick up the ball and nobody complained because he always paid the caddies and bought the drinks afterward."

Back in the locker room the Colonel would break into his deep bass voice in the shower and the others would join in. Bill Street described the friendly atmosphere of those days. "That was one great thing about the old club. Everyone knew everyone else. Anyone could go out there anytime and get a golf game. It was just one of those kinds of things. . . ."

It was the Colonel who was the symbol of "those kinds of things." One of the additions to the club during his presidency was the appearance of the *Club Times* in June 1938, the brainchild of William Burckel. One of the first articles carried this profile of Colonel Bob:

Continued on page 67

ATLANTA ATHLETIC CLUB

CLUB **TIMES**

EAST LAKE COUNTRY CLUB

ORGANIZED SEPTEMBER 1898 FOR "ENJOYING PHYSICAL EXERCISE"

Vol. IX, No. 2   ATLANTA, GEORGIA   September 8, 1950

Welcome:

W. B. FARNSWORTH, president of the East Lake Country Club and Atlanta Athletic Club, extends the following welcome—as chairman of the Reception Committee—in the opening pages of the Official Program for the Golden Anniversary Women's Amateur Golf Championship:

"We who are members of the Atlanta Athletic Club are honored to have you, whether as contestant or spectator, visit the East Lake Country Club—the cradle of champions—for the fiftieth Women's Amateur Golf Championship of the United States Golf Association.

"We consider it a great privilege to extend hospitality to America's golf and country club leaders, if only in exchange for that enjoyed so often elsewhere by East Lake's noted golfers—Bob Jones, Alexa Stirling, Charlie Yates, Watts Gunn and others. Our committees have planned and worked eagerly to arrange facilities and accommodations worthy of our distinguished guests.

"We hope you will be so pleased that this Golden Anniversary Women's Championship of the U.S.G.A. will be but the first of many feature events which you will enjoy with us."

PRESIDENT W. B. (Bip) Farnsworth, left, congratulates T. R. (Dick) Garlington, AAC Board Chairman, on securing USGA's Women's Tournament for East Lake.

The Trophy for the USGA Women's Amateur Golf Championship will be on display in a Davison's department store window until September 10. Then it will be on display in the East Lake Clubhouse for a week.

Hail to USGA and the Ladies!

Because the East Lake Country Club is so highly honored by the playing of the Golden Anniversary Women's Amateur Golf Championship of the United States Golf Association here this month, we have incorporated in this special September issue of the AAC CLUB TIMES pictures, features, and news suitable to the occasion.

We hope every AAC member will find this issue of extra help and interest as we welcome the United States Golf Association officials, contestants, and spectators.

THE EDITOR.

The Prize

To have and to hold this handsome cup is the reward to the annual winner of the Women's Amateur Golf Championship of the United States Golf Association. The defending champion, Mrs. Mark A. Porter, proudly displays it to her daughter.

Since this championship trophy was presented to USGA in 1896 by Robert Cox, of Gorgie, Edinburgh, Scotland, a golfer and graduate of St. Andrew's, it has been won and held by more than 30 women, including two Atlantans—Miss Alexa Stirling (now Mrs. W. G. Fraser, Ottawa, Canada), and Miss Louise Suggs. Miss Stirling won the cup three times!

The cup itself is a vase of Etruscan design, about 24 inches high and 10 inches in diameter. The vase is treated in enamel that bears scenes of St. Andrew's. It is delicately and artfully designed, with silver plates showing the names of the winners.

"Follow Through To Help Others"

That is the title of the official program for the Golden Anniversary Women's Amateur Golf Championship of the United States Golf Association, which will be played at the East Lake Country Club, September 11-16.

The reason for this theme of "helpfulness" is that the new Atlanta Cerebral Palsy School at 1815 Ponce de Leon Avenue, N.E., will receive the profits from the sale of all the programs. The organization, plans, and purposes for training cerebral-palsied children are explained in the program.

One of the most complete and colorful programs ever published for the annual women's amateur tournament, this 1950 edition takes a backward glance at the history of women's golf, the championship winners, outstanding tournaments and golfers at East Lake. The program includes a hole-by-hole

Robert Purmedus Jones (with T.R. Garlington, Pres. 1947), affectionately known as "Colonel Bob," personified the upbeat spirit of the club life during the growth years between the depression and World War II.

He likes to sing bass in the shower room; he likes people; he cusses in a manner that is musical and artistic and not at all offensive. He can question a man's ancestry and make it feel like a caress. He can create loyalty and devotion. . . . They've got most of us in a mold — a few they can't get in. A few remain out. They are the men with the real personality. They are the men whom people love and follow. The Colonel is one of those . . . . He is a part of the soul of East Lake Club; one of the personalities who kept us going as something more than just brick and stone and lake and green and fairway.

Hugh Dorsey, who was a partner in Colonel Jones' law firm, adds his own footnote to this plaudit: "A lot of people can cuss, but without the music it's just profanity. He had the music."

Colonel Jones resigned from the presidency in 1942, giving the reins to Henry Heinz. He returned to the board of directors, where he served a total of 38 years (1908-1946), the longest tenure of any member in the club. His son Bobby served on the board from 1928 through 1947, and served the club as president in 1946.

Other Activities at East Lake

While golfing was the center of activity during the thirties and forties, East Lake was also popular for non-golfing activities, particularly swimming. One of East Lake's swimmers, Louise Roberts, became a member of the 1932 Olympic team, stimulating interest in the sport. And in 1938 Fred Lanoue came to East Lake (where he would fill Joe Bean's shoes until 1942), bringing with him an increased emphasis on water sports and safety. With the waterfront open from 10:00 a.m. until 7:00 p.m., he taught his swimming classes a technique he had developed called "drownproofing," which enabled swimmers to remain afloat indefinitely with little effort.

Lanoue also brought a carnival atmosphere to the waterfront on holidays, particularly for the annual water show, importing all sorts of bizarre acts to stimulate interest in water sports. There were Catfish Charlie, who attempted to break the world's record for staying underwater; Jerry the Gristleman, who towed a rowboat loaded with six people while his hands and feet were bound; Abdullah the Bohemian, who would race all comers in the water; John Hiles, who drank a bottle of Coke underwater; and Bob Roberts, who ate a banana underwater, to name a fantastic few.

As bizarre as Lanoue's shows were, he succeeded in increasing attendance in his swimming and physical education classes. He was particularly successful in encouraging women to become active

While swimming was a popular East Lake activity, some girls would rather polish their dance steps.

The forties brought an increased interest in water sports and recreation at East Lake.

The younger set kicked up a storm for their instructors at East Lake.

in athletics. In his classes he was almost tyrannical, shouting commands and driving the women to their limits. To the surprise of their male counterparts, they loved the demanding atmosphere, rewarding Lanoue with loyal attendance and even gifts.

As women and children became more involved in the club's athletic program, the emphasis continued to shift away from team sports toward individual sports and fitness. "This pool and many of the other facilities are available to the wives and daughters of members on certain days each week," wrote W. A. Alexander in the *Club Times* in September 1938. "At other times classes for boys are held, with instructions in swimming, diving, wrestling, and boxing; with still other hours set apart for girls. Thus, there is something for each member of the family, not only to interest and amuse, but also to build and maintain sturdy health."

When Fred Lanoue left East Lake to become the swimming coach at Georgia Tech in 1942, the club hired Ed Shea to take his place. Shea's first article for the *Club Times* indicated that he, too, felt responsible for more than simply the competitive sports. "The teaching of Physical Education, which formerly was considered a matter of teaching a few competitive sports or gym exercises, has come to involve a broad range of human interests and activities," he wrote, "and on the basis of this newer outlook, I believe we may go forward with a program of personal interest to all of you."

Another trend that contributed to the shift away from team sports at the club was the increased sponsorship of these sports by colleges. "We had had volleyball teams and basketball teams," remembers Edwin Baumer, a member of the club's wrestling team in the 1930s. "All of a sudden it was dead. All that activity was taken over by the colleges."

Individual sports continued to be popular, and Jim Carlton (chairman of the tennis committee) and Sam Carstarphen (the club's tennis pro) kept the six courts at East Lake busy in the late 1940s. John Ager was one of the club's leading tennis competitors at the time.

About a year after Lanoue left, Joe Bean returned to his old job at the Athletic Club and remained there until his retirement in 1950, giving the club a total of 35 years of service. (He served as consultant and coach when John T. Foster became physical director on September 15, 1949.) He knew as well as any that the era of Bean's Boys was ended, and he became a strong advocate of individual physical fitness.

It was during this time (1942) that Jimmy Fischer was hired as manager, and he and his wife Mildred brought new emphasis to the club's din-

It was a time of inner tubes in the water, playpens on the lawn, and lazy hours chatting with friends.

ing facilities. His years in hotel and club management had prepared him well to increase the interest in East Lake's facilities. Soon he was providing lavish Sunday buffets, and Saturday night dinner dances featured well-known orchestras, such as Johnny Miller, Frank Patrick, and Bob Lucas. Even on weekdays, the dining room at East Lake was often filled, and the club enjoyed a reputation of being one of the pleasantest spots in Atlanta for dining.

Life at Carnegie Way

Meanwhile, Carnegie Way's dining facilities were enjoying the same increased patronage as membership grew: diners filled the Crystal Room on special menu nights, such as lobster night, oyster night, and international night; businessmen and shoppers made lunchtime a bustling period for the staff; the Highlander Room was booked with bridal and debutante parties; on fall weekends there were football brunches; and in the summer the roof garden was a favorite Atlanta gathering place. "We never missed a Saturday night when they built the roof garden," claimed Bill Street. "We had some great times there. There would be 45 to 50 at one table. Everybody knew everybody. . . . They had an orchestra every night — downstairs in the winter and on the roof garden in the summer. It was a beautiful spot." Alva Maxwell agrees: "AAC was the most popular eating place downtown for years and years."

Other facilities at Carnegie Way were also in high demand. "We used to have a lot of parties, particularly house parties for the Chevrolet company," remembers Mary Happoldt. "Alton Costly was a manager for Chevrolet at the time and brought all of their business to the club. They used to have automobile shows down there in the gym. . . . They brought the cars up through the back entrance, where the old Lyric Theatre was."

The athletic facilities at Carnegie Way were also busy. Badminton had been growing in popularity since the mid-1930s and was fast becoming the most popular sport in the country. "You couldn't walk down the streets in Atlanta without seeing three outdoor courts on every block," says A. E. "Pat" Patton. Club interest was heightened when member W. C. "Cam" Mitchell won the singles titles both in the City Badminton Championship and in the Southern Y.M.C.A. Championship in 1939.

Patton became a Wednesday night regular in the late 1930s, sometimes waiting for hours for a chance to play. William "Bill" Braswell caught the badminton bug shortly after he joined in 1941, when Mary Staton whipped him badly in his first

W.C. "Cam" Mitchell heightened the club's interest in badminton when he won the singles titles in the City Championship and the southern YMCA Championship in 1939. L — R: Bill Rocker, Allen McGhee, Dallas Thompson, Cam Mitchell.

Johnny Ager (left) and Allen Hardin (right) led the play in the newly popular game of badminton.

game at the club. "I didn't even score on her!" he exclaims, still remembering his dismay. "I'd played backyard badminton and thought I was pretty good, but I didn't even score. I said, 'I'm going to learn to play this game!'"

World War II dampened interest in the game somewhat, with blackouts eliminating outdoor play at night and younger members being drafted. But badminton remained popular through the 1940s, with such players as Allen Hardin and Johnny Ager leading the play. In 1949 Hardin won the Southern men's singles crown at the Southern Badminton Association tournament. And Cam Mitchell and Pat Patton, now proficient, took the men's doubles championship the same year. In succeeding years, these players were to win many of the same titles repeatedly.

A core group of seven — Pat Patton, Bill Braswell, Cam Mitchell, William P. "Bill" Rocker, Allen "Al" McGhee, Winfrey "Breezy" Wynn, and James "Jim" Taylor — continued to play avidly through the forties and fifties, developing a strong camaraderie. Braswell and Taylor proved to be such an unbeatable combination they were prohibited from playing together in the club's annual Turkey Tournament at Thanksgiving.

In 1959 Taylor, in high spirits from a windfall on the stock market, decided to give the group official status. At a special luncheon he announced the formation of the Royal and Ancient Kingdom of the Seven Cats' Eyes, presenting each of the other six with a cat's-eye ring and soberly advising them, "Later, by diligent deeds you may even become a Pole Cat, if so elected." From that time Taylor was known as "Chief Polecat," Patton as "Prowling Cat," Mitchell as "Hepcat," Braswell as "Swingcat," Rocker as "Tomcat," and McGhee as "Squarecat." The group continued to play through the sixties, hosting the Southern Badminton championships at the Carnegie Way club in 1962. They presented Taylor with six silver goblets in 1966, prompting an article in the November 20 *Atlanta Journal* entitled "Order of Seven Cat's Eyes Watch the Birdies Fly." (Some members of the group continue to play together today.)

"A Most Valuable Asset"

It was a grand era for the Athletic Club — growing membership, good management (at East Lake in Jimmy Fischer and at Carnegie Way in Albert Happoldt), and a time in history when a club filled a special need in Atlanta. In October 1938 Mayor William B. Hartsfield wrote a promotional article for the *Club Times* that describes the importance he placed on club membership during those years. "Atlanta has for many years been a

Bob Lassiter shakes opponent Dallas Thompson's hand after winning the club's singles championship.

club town and many of our citizens have centered their social life in their club, seldom entertaining at home," he wrote. "Business organizations use club facilities for their meetings and banquets. Civic drives of general interest arrange for headquarters and pep meetings, civic clubs meet, visiting notables are entertained and in every way imaginable our clubs hold the interest of our citizens. It is, therefore, apparent that a club membership is a most valuable asset, and to a man who cares to enter into the activities of our community, a positive necessity. The modern home of the Atlanta Athletic Club offers such a wide field of activity for its members, that, once included in its membership, one wonders how he previously got along."

The same situation was true in the next decade. "When I joined the club [in 1947] the social life of the people in Atlanta revolved around their home and their club," remembers J. W. Jones. "There were no 'restaurants,' so-called — the type that we have today. There was no place to go at night. The hotels had dining rooms, but clubs were used as an extension of a home. On the cook's night off, you went to the club for dinner. The Woodruffs entertained a great deal at the club. If they were entertaining, they went to a club; they didn't do it at their home. . . . The reputation of the Athletic Club was, of course, first-class. It was and still is one of the premier clubs."

With the increase in members came gradual relief from the enormous indebtedness of the club at the onset of the Depression. At $250 to join ($100 to buy a share of stock and $150 to pay the initiation fee) and $16 a month (for golfing members) in 1948, membership in AAC was apparently considered a good value. By 1943 long-term debt had been reduced from a high of $934,000 to $805,000. By 1948 that figure had dropped to around $300,000 and the club had accumulated in cash and government bonds about $650,000. The Athletic Club was again in the black, its growth fed by the undiminished fame of Bobby Jones and the more recent successes of Tommy Barnes and Charlie Yates.

Boosted by such charismatic leaders as Colonel Bob Jones, spirits were up once again. But they were tempered spirits of a society that had tasted a Depression. The club would boldly pursue new dreams in the future, as it had fifty years before when it was founded on Edgewood Avenue. But it would never again do so with the unalloyed fearlessness of its earliest days.

Chapter Ten

The 1950s, Halcyon Years

By the 1950s it was apparent that a demographic change was reshaping Atlanta. Population growth was shifting to the north of the city — toward Marietta, Sandy Springs, Roswell, Dunwoody, and Stone Mountain, the string of prosperous suburban towns along the city's perimeter that would later be dubbed the "Golden Crescent." As many of AAC's members joined this northward migration, they began to pose the idea of a northside golf course for AAC. It was the foreshadowing of a painful transition for the club that would ultimately wrench it from its established place in downtown Atlanta and place it at the outer rim of Atlanta's northward expansion.

But, for the 1950s, the club maintained a kind of equilibrium in its geography, investing both in northside facilities and southside facilities. The idea of a northside course was still in its infancy, but another type of northside facility did become a reality.

The Yacht Club

In the early part of the decade, the U.S. Corps of Engineers announced plans to build a dam north of Atlanta, impounding the waters of the Chattahoochee and Chestatee Rivers. The announcement caught the attention of AAC members who had moved to the north side of Atlanta, and they began to talk of a yacht club at the proposed 39,000-acre lake, which was to be called Lake Sidney Lanier.

The idea struck the leadership of the club as a good compromise, according to Charles Elliott. 'At that time, a whispered campaign was underway to establish a third golf course somewhere north of Atlanta, within easier access than the two East Lake courses, to many members who lived on the north side . . . the country club facility was concentrated around the clubhouse for a compact and manageable unit, and the majority of ranking members who ran AAC thought that two widely separated golf facilities would spread the operation too thin and cost more money than the club could afford.''

Ira H. Hardin, who joined the board in 1953, was given the task of scouting out the 6 or 7 miles of future shoreline for a good site — one that was scenic and accessible and that had deep enough water to support a boating facility. He found two good sites — one was a long, sloping hillside that had been farmland on the Big Creek side of the lake; and the other was a deep, wooded cove on the mainland, near the mouth of Flowery Branch Creek.

Dick (T.R.) Garlington, accompanied by another member, Eugene Brooks, attended an auction for the properties around the lake and bought options for both sites, acting as agent for AAC. (Both sites were part of the estate of A. H. Holland.) The club decided to locate the facility on the Flowery Branch site and eventually exchanged the other site for additional property adjacent to the Flowery Branch location. A later purchase brought AAC's total acreage there to 50.

The Charles M. Graves Co., landscape architects, created the plans for the facility, which would include docks, a launching ramp, a grill and restroom facility, a picnic area, and a large parking lot.

The club tapped one of its existing employees, William H. "Bud" Walters, to manage the construction phases for the new facility. A tall and stout man, Walters had grown up in nearby Toccoa and was familiar not only with the mountainous type of land at Lake Lanier, but also with the ways of the north Georgia people who would be involved in construction and maintenance of the facility. He had joined the Carnegie Way maintenance department in 1947 with a background in refrigeration and had gone to East Lake when the clubhouse was air-conditioned in 1952. There he soon became manager of maintenance for the country club.

At the Yacht Club, his first order of business was to get the ramp extended into the still-low waters so the eager club members could make use

Right from the start the Yacht Club was a big success. It opened with one dock (and eight berths) in 1958 and by 1961 it was docking more than 100 boats.

of the facility. By the fall of 1957 the ramp, access road, and parking lot had been completed.

Right from the start the Yacht Club was a big success. Walters had scarcely poured the concrete before AACers with boats and trailers had arrived at the ramp to launch their fishing boats and scout the newly created lake. Walters found himself not only managing construction, but a demanding operation as well. On top of the fishers and pleasure boaters came so many picnickers that members covered the hillside on weekends, looking to Walters to help them locate and set up grills, tables, trash containers, and toilet facilities. Walters' construction crews were conscripted for service in coping with the crowds. The makeshift restrooms, a reminder of the outhouses of yesteryear, prompted some on-the-spot history lessons for the younger generation.

Gradually, the facilities took shape. First the docks. "The Yacht Club committee made a reconnaissance of the boat docks on Lanier as well as on a number of other older lakes, talked with some of the larger companies in the business and decided on the best boat docks then available," writes Elliott. "With styrofoam floats, heavy docks were put up to stay. All were anchored with cables in such a manner that they could be shifted out and then back to the shoreline with the fluctuations of the water level." Before the first docks were completed, the list of boaters applying for berths was twice as long as the eight spaces available. "Lanier Yacht Club was popular even before it got in operation," marvels Elliott. "Each dock was filled as it was built, and one spot on the hill had to be set aside for storage of boats and trailers."

The next facility constructed was a snack bar with restrooms, high on the knoll looking over the entire marina area and out on the increasingly beautiful lake set into north Georgia's mountains. It was formally opened in July 1958: "The crowd was so large that a number of members put on aprons, helped to cook and served as waiters, and before it was over the stock of food and drink . . . had run out to the last cracker. But the spirit of that day, with its flow of fellowship, gave an indication of the huge success AAC's Lanier Yacht Club was to enjoy," says Elliott.

The social program of the new AAC club was largely informal, with members cruising together by day and swapping boat visits with their neighbors along the docks during the late afternoon and evening. But the Yacht Club also became known for four social events. Two were for the overall AAC membership — a July Fourth Barbecue and a Labor Day Country Dinner and Square Dance. And two were for Yacht Club members only — a Cast-Off Party to inaugurate the spring boating season and a Shipwreck Party in the fall to mark the on-

coming winter season. "They were great parties," remembered Bill Street. "We used to have bands come out there, and the dock we called the 'party dock' used to party all night long."

In 1962 the Yacht Club was organized into a formal unit, with its own officers, headed by a "commodore," who was chairman of the Yacht Club committee. When Glenn Dewberry became commodore of the Yacht Club in 1971, succeeding Oliver Saggus, he started a few other club traditions. "We got real formal," he remembers fondly. "We put up a big mast and would fly the flags of the commodore or second commodore when they were in — that is, when we remembered to follow the rules."

By the end of 1966, membership in the Yacht Club had grown from a handful to more than 200. Boating facilities included 51 open dock spaces, 36 houseboat slips, 58 covered dock spaces, 10 dry storage areas, and a parking lot for boats on trailers. Entertainment facilities included an outdoor picnic area, enlarged snack bar, television lounge, and pavilion.

Eugene Brooks was one of many members involved in the early days of the Yacht Club.

In 1950 the club enlarged the porch at East Lake to provide a terrace for dancing. The moonlit Saturday night dances were extremely popular.

As the Yacht Club began to be the center of many club members' lives, they developed a real affection and appreciation for Bud Walters and his wife Jimmie (who was employed as restaurant manager), and for Bob Bell, who served as facility manager. Walters not only kept up with the food operation, but managed the maintenance of the grounds, managed the ramps and docks, and managed the special events. "Suggest anything to be done up there and he would say, 'I'll do it,'" says Gene Brooks. "He could do anything." One night Walters spent the entire night searching the lake for a member and his wife, who was pregnant, only to find later they had forgotten to tell him of their plans to spend the night at a friend's house on the lake. "Bud Walters was a great manager," says Dewberry. "He worked and really developed the facility. He was about 58 years old at the time of the expansion in 1969 and retired [in 1976] at about 65."

Top AAC Swimmers

While the Athletic Club was investing in this engaging new facility on the north side, its East Lake and Carnegie Way clubs continued to be popular.

With the increased interest in dining at East Lake, the club decided in 1950 to enlarge the porch to provide a terrace for dancing and to move

Charles Cooper and Mrs. J. H. Shepherd proudly stand with the beginners' swimming class in May 1955. L-R, 1st row: Terry Ethier, Susan Ridenour, Karen Roach, Leigh Waters, Joanne Backer. 2nd: Lynne Bishop, James Shepherd, Dana Shepherd, Mike Ethier, Ricky Angel, Billy Ethier. 3: Barbara Backer, Susanne Huffman, Margie Gregory, Vicky Ison, Shelby Mills, Lynne Gregory, Susan LaShanna. 4th: Chas. Cooper, Mrs. J. H. Shepherd, Paul Bishop, Jerry Mills, Tommy English, Tommy Albright, Tommy Waldrop, Andy Andrews. Not in picture: David & Warren Earl, Jon Braswell, Billy Bowen, Jenky Richards, Mrs. Chas. Bowen, Dan & Mynel Yates.

In 1958 East Lake built a swimming pool that was the largest and finest in the city.

the men's locker room from the second to the ground floor. The new wing, 100 by 160 feet, was designed by architects Stevens and Wilkerson and built by J. A. Jones Construction Company. The new locker room contained two sets of showers and 820 lockers, with the golf shop and the men's grill adjacent to the locker room.

"The night they opened the terrace they sold every table and every place they could find," remembers Charles Ponder. "They had this big orchestra called the Dean Hudson Orchestra. It was one of the favorite orchestras in the country. It looked like it was going to rain all day, and I wasn't planning to go but I got a table right up against the wall. About the time he started his music the bottom dropped out of the sky. It didn't rain. It just came down like something that had just dropped. Everybody rushed down into the locker room. We had a wonderful time. You got acquainted with people you didn't know."

After the success of the new dance floor at East Lake, in 1954 the club remodeled the roof garden at Carnegie Way, which had lapsed into disuse. The "garden" was filled with plantings — dwarf magnolias, loquats, petunias, and coleus — and surrounded by a black wrought iron fence,

The club's female swimmers of the 1950s, including Mary "Liz" Davison, were top-flight national competitors.

Charles Cooper presents a trophy to Nancy Ivey.

Charles A. Cooper, Jr., hired as athletic director in 1952, was an immediate hit with both children and adults. L — R: Mr. Edward Adams, Mrs. Adams, Charles Cooper, Tubby (Bob) Adams, Butch (Dick) Adams.

79

A beaming group welcomes the new year with bells on.

The younger set sports behive hairstyles and three-button jackets.

to match the chairs and glass-topped tables. The dance floor was highly polished. An orchestra played every summer evening except Sunday, from 7:00 to 11:00. (Jimmy Gonzales and his Latin American band were favorites.) And again it became a favorite gathering place for Atlanta society and the scene of many debutante parties. As the winter chill set in, dancing moved into the gym (Al Doonan Hall) to the tunes of famous bands such as Sammy Kaye and his orchestra, Les Brown and his Band of Renown, and Guy Lombardo and his orchestra.

In athletics, too, the two clubs were the scene of a new kind of excitement. Harry Glancy, AAC member and former member of the 1924-1928 Olympic swimming team, had built strong interest in the sport in Atlanta. Like Harold Sargent, he was one of the founders of the Havalanta games, which included competition between young swimmers from Atlanta and Havana, Cuba.

As a result of his high profile, a generation of talented female swimmers grew up at AAC, swimming at East Lake in the summer months and at the Carnegie Way club in the winters. In a February 1942 article in the *Club Times*, Ed Shea had commented, "That swimming pool of ours [at Carnegie way] has been turned into a regular laboratory, workshop, for the youngsters, out of which should come promising material for the future."

That prediction was accurate. By the 1950s the talent was obvious, particularly among the female swimmers. Under the eye of, first, John Foster as athletic director; then Don Casady, acting director when Foster was called to active duty in the navy in 1950; then Phil Cady, who became athletic director in June 1951, the club had one of the most competitive female swim teams in the Southeast. In 1950, for instance, 14-year-old Penny Barnett won the national junior 220 freestyle event at the Southeastern Amateur Athletic Union (AAU) meet in Birmingham, Alabama. At the same meet the AAC relay team of Mary Davison, Catherine Turner, Jo Holland, and Elaine Fladger set a new record for the 220 freestyle relay. These girls, joined by Gail Benton, Sandra Benton, and Mary Link, were Atlanta's topflight swimmers of the era.

In 1954 Gail Benton and Jo Holland proved that their talents were national-level by winning second places in the national AAU meet in Daytona, Florida — the first time a member of any Georgia team had placed so high in national competition.

To maintain this high standard in swimming, in 1952 the club hired as athletic director Charles A. Cooper, Jr., a former University of Georgia

swim team captain, all-American freestyle swimmer, and winner of three Southeastern Conference championships in swimming. Cooper was immediately a hit, not only in swimming, but in other sports. "He had camps for the children and would keep them involved all day long," remembers Jean (Mrs. Eugene) Brooks.

To stimulate interest in tennis, he appointed Bill Doeg as tennis pro. He also encouraged golf pro Harold Sargent to instruct youngsters on specified days, as his father had done.

East Lake soon found that its lake facilities were being strained from the increased number of swimmers, boaters, and fishers. The beach was overcrowded, the locker rooms were overcrowded,

Continued on page 84

East Lake Grill Room. Hal Cook and wife, head table.

The fifties were times when luaus and shipwreck parties set the tone for club life.

A ladies lunch at the club was a full-dress occasion, often including a hat.

The board of directors for 1954-1955 included (L-R) George C. Munn, Hugh M. Dorsey, Jr. (President), Watts Gunn (Chairman), and William Leide. Berrien Moore, Jr (Director) not in picture.

Bill Daly, son of Mr. and Mrs. M. T. Daly shows what a twist of the wrist can do.

Paul Runyon (pro) offers a few tips to Dr. Harry W. Ridley (kneeling) and Travis Johnson.

Continued from page 83

swimmers complained about the chemicals used to treat the lake for fishing, and management conceded that the lake was no longer as pollution-free as it had been.

In 1957 the board of directors decided to build a swimming pool, to be designed by J. Wylly Keck, Jr. & Associates of Atlanta and Tony Shennan and Associates of Miami. When it was opened in June 1958, the members found it was the largest and finest swimming facility in the city, and perhaps in the South. It was 164 feet long, fitted with underwater lights, and surrounded by a grass terrace, snack bar, and bathhouse.

Cooper took advantage of the new facility to step up water activities. He immediately began offering swimming classes and scheduled meets with other clubs in the city. In 1961 he hired Carlos de Cubas, a renowned Cuban swimming and diving coach (who had fled Cuba when Communist forces took control in 1960), and, to help with the swimming program in the summers, a Westminster Schools instructor and former UGA fraternity brother, Wiley R. "Buz" McGriff.

When Cooper left the Athletic Club in 1962 to become manager of a club in South Carolina, after a decade as athletic director, he left a legacy of young people of both sexes who would remain active in the club's athletic programs. His successor was Buz McGriff.

The fishers, meanwhile, reveled in their now-exclusive claim to the lake. The dock facilities were improved and the old clubhouse on the lake, which actually predated the existence of the country club, was removed.

The Mingledorff Era

These good times for the Athletic Club, with facilities being expanded at East Lake and Carnegie Way and a new facility built at Lake Lanier, were the fruits of growth in the late 1940s, when membership had risen to more than 3,000. They were also the fruits of good management, which ran the extensive operations of the club in a way that generated high use by members and, therefore, a surplus of funds for expansion. When Albert Happold resigned in 1946, after nearly two decades of service (to manage the Highlands Country Club, in which Scott Hudson was a principal investor), he was soon succeeded by Clyde Mingledorff, who had joined the club in 1943 as auditor/secretary (John Riley was general manager for one year.)

Mingledorff was regarded as an evenhanded and personable manager by club members. He adhered closely to the principles he had learned from Scott Hudson — "run a tight ship and remember that you're an employee." That philosophy earned him not only the admiration of club members and appointment as general manager in 1951, but the admiration of his peers as well; in 1956 he was elected president of the national Club Managers Association.

The fifties were an excellent time to be associated with the Athletic Club, a halcyon time when the depression years had been forgotten and the stresses of the next decade were not yet upon the club.

Chapter Eleven

Adapting to Change

*G*radually, almost imperceptibly at first, the social changes in Atlanta, shifting growth to the north, began to erode the popularity of East Lake Country Club. Attendance at the Sunday buffets declined, particularly after Jimmy Fischer resigned in 1962; the moonlight dances lost their magic; and the foursomes no longer lingered at the men's grill after their play. Though the members were not yet fully aware of their significance, the changes signaled the beginning of the end for East Lake as a member of the AAC family. And the transition would be painful for the club's members.

The board's initial response was to redecorate and improve the facilities. The number one course, as mentioned earlier, was extensively renovated for the 1963 British-American Ryder Cup Match, bringing it into its finest condition ever. And the interior of the grand Tudor clubhouse was refurbished. But the efforts were to little avail.

One barometer of the social changes in the neighborhood was the increase in vandalism. In September 1962 the *Club Times* reported that vandalism on our two courses cost the club approximately $1,000 [during a four-month period]. This money went to replace markers on the tees, repair broken benches, replace flags and flagpoles which were stolen or wrapped around a nearby tree, repair mutilated ball washers and drinking fountains, and in some cases replacing a section of green dug up or otherwise damaged by the prowlers." The club eventually erected a fence around the clubhouse and the number one course. The number two course, still vulnerable, continued to suffer regular damage.

Uneasy about the safety of the neighborhood, many members began to avoid East Lake. "The membership had stopped supporting anything," remembers Jean Brooks. "The golfers would come out, and in the summer the swimmers would come out. But they weren't supporting anything socially in the club. They said it was too far away." The Brookses, like many other AAC families, had

moved from a nearby community (Decatur) to north Atlanta in the early 1960s.

"As fine as East Lake was, it was clear that was not where the future was going to be. The geo-

In the 1960s, meetings of the members often led to serious debates about the club's future.

graphical center of the membership of the club was no longer there," says Hugh M. Dorsey, Jr., who, as president of the club from 1955 to 1957, began to look for a new location for the country club toward the end of his term. It was the central issue for the presidents who followed him — Ira H. Hardin, W. L. Clifton, Jr., F. M. "Buster" Bird, and H. C. "Hikie" Allen, Jr.

In 1963 President Hikie Allen quietly assembled a committee to explore the options for relocating the country club. Buster Bird, a member of the committee, suggested they retain Hammer, Siler, Green to study the demographics of Atlanta. "We asked them to draw a circle around the area on the map that was most appropriate for a country club for the next 25 years," remembers Bird. "The circle they drew came as no surprise. It was in the fast-growing crescent between highways 75 and 85 on the north side." Atlanta developer Scott Hudgens, Jr., acquired three options for the club, and after considering the three sites, the board of directors decided on 617 pine-covered acres in Fulton County, along a bend in the Chattahoochee River. The board bought the property from Ben Summerour for $429,836 and appointed Jim Shumate (later replaced by Oliver Saggus), Watts Gunn, and Allen Hardin to oversee development plans for a golf course and clubhouse.

East Lake Is Sold

For those close to the situation, the purchase signaled a major change for the club. "The die had been cast, just by that," Clyde Mingledorff remembers thinking as he walked the property lines. "One of these days East Lake was gonna go as excess baggage. We couldn't afford a country club both north and east."

At first, the actions of the board were tolerated by the members who were loyal to East Lake, on the assumption that a northside course would be an additional facility. But tension mounted as they began to perceive the likely outcome. "When the sentiment developed to the point of suggesting that East Lake Country Club itself be supplanted by a northside installation, the lid blew off," remembers Charles Elliott, himself an East Lake advocate at the time. "Members who lived in Decatur and the northeast section of Atlanta made up almost as large a percentage of the membership as the northsiders, and the club arrayed itself as two factions who took opposite sides of the issue. One argument was that the rich tradition built up around East Lake over almost two-thirds of a century would be violated, leaving AAC just another normal, run-of-the-mill athletic club."

Nevertheless, the majority of the stockholders voted in March 1966 to sell the number two golf course to finance development at "River Bend." Feeling ran so high that when potential buyers (represented by Alex Smith) stipulated it had to be rezoned for housing development, some of the members loyal to East Lake tried to influence the county zoning board to deny the petition. The rezoning was accomplished, however, and the sale brought the club $1,000,000.

For two years members debated whether or not to sell the remainder of the East Lake property, confirming the worst fears of those who lived near the club. In the meantime, the board refurbished both the remaining East Lake course and the clubhouse in an effort to make the country club viable. "The old No. 1 course at East Lake was put into the finest condition of its existence," writes Elliott. "And, in an attempt to reattract the luncheon and dinner crowds, much of the interior of the attractive English Tudor-style club house was redecorated. In addition, the men's grill was converted into a trophy room, with members donating the prized specimens of their prowess, as beautifully mounted marlin, sailfish, tarpon and a number of unusual game animals for the walls. Best chefs and waiters available were obtained and high quality food prepared. Special services were inaugurated, such as bus service between the club and baseball and football games. The club went all out to keep East Lake a going concern, but in spite of all efforts, use of the facility, except for the golf play, fell off, and the club continued deeper into the red." Swimming participation, for example, dropped from 15,000 in 1966 to 10,000 in 1967, according to the *Club Times*.

The board was ready to sell. In a February 1968 report, President Larry P. Martin wrote, "I believe that this club can live with only one golf facility, unless we want to pay substantially higher golfing dues than at present. If and when the Board calls a special stockholders' meeting with a specific recommendation, the stockholders will have an opportunity to approve or disapprove it. I believe that it will be at River Bend, in the path of the future rather than in the past, which cannot be changed."

On April 2, 1968, the stockholders voted 900 in favor of selling East Lake and 551 opposed. A bitter battle involving a lawsuit followed, and ultimately 25 members — including Paul R. Grigsby, Tommy Barnes, Bill Liede, and Charles Elliott pooled their resources to buy the property themselves (at a price of $1.8 million), opening their own club and splitting in two the Athletic Club's membership.

The break that had been so long in coming had finally been made. "Having been one who had occupied one of the positions of responsibility — knowing that it had to be done but not being able

The interior of the East Lake clubhouse was refurbished in the early 1960s, in an effort to rekindle interest in the club.

to figure out how it could be done — I have great respect for those who did it, especially Buster," says Hugh Dorsey, Jr. "He took most of the flak, of which there was a good deal."

A Struggling Athletic Program

Throughout these trials, the management of East Lake tried to provide a good athletic and social program. But there, too, the times had caught up with them, in a different way. McGriff continued the emphasis Cooper had placed on family participation and individual sports, among other things offering a popular mom-and-tot swim class, judo, and weightlifting. And de Cubas' swimming program continued to produce fine athletes. "Coach De Cubas has made the Atlanta Athletic Club's swimming team the greatest in the south," boasted the September 1966 *Club Times*. "Georgia swimmers acquired 801.5 points against North

Carolina's 321.5, South Carolina's 232 points, and Alabama, Tennessee, and North Florida's total of 404 points. The Atlanta Athletic Club swimmers acquired half of the points for the state of Georgia in the regional meet."

But the shift in the structure of athletics across the U.S. that Edwin Baumer had noticed in the 1940s had caught up with AAC. As other institutions — particularly the colleges — began to develop strong programs in swimming, basketball, and other sports, the AAU competition got tougher. "We didn't have enough talented swimmers and divers anymore," says McGriff. "We had a few — like Susie Matthews, Billy Heinz, Jr. (who was invited to try out for the Olympic diving team), Lee Bradford (an all-American high school swimmer), and Julie Ginden. But not enough. We decided to compete just within the Inter-Club League." Basketball, handball, squash, volleyball, and badminton games continued in the Carnegie Way gym,

Joe McCurey and Bill Braswell shape up for the Southern Badminton Championships in 1968.

Volleyball players in the 1967 "Turkey Tournament" included L — R: Wade Seal, Carl Mankin, —, —, Bob   *Wester, Jim Creech, —, Warn Carah, Ed Henderson, —.*

with club championships in January and February, and the Turkey Tournament in November. But interest was not high.

The one activity that attracted increasing interest was racquetball. "The guy who invented the game, Joe Soebeck, came cold to my office about 1966," recalls McGriff. "He said, 'I've got a game I think you'll be interested in.' He had a racquet like a sawed-off tennis racket and a blue ball about the size of a tennis ball. He called the game 'paddle racquets.' We started playing paddle racquets and began to get a little following."

But, in general, interest in athletics was ebbing at AAC. "We had grown soft," concludes McGriff in retrospect. "We were golf and social. Athletics wasn't part of the thinking. I was taking the horse to water, but the horse didn't want to drink. I seriously considered taking another job."

A Proud Structure Crumbles

The sale of East Lake was not to be the only loss the Athletic Club would suffer within a decade. In 1973 an event occurred that shook not only the membership but many other citizens of Atlanta: the Carnegie Way club was dynamited to make way for a new hotel.

Albert and Mary Happoldt (who had left the club in 1946, after 18 years of service) were driving through Atlanta and, unaware the destruction was to take place, witnessed the scene. Their feelings mirror those of others that day. "We were on the way to Florida, coming up Spring Street on a Sunday, and I saw the roof cave in," recalls Mary Happoldt quietly. The 10-story structure, designed by Philip Shutze, crumbled efficiently into itself, roof garden upon Crystal Room, upon gymnasium. In little more than 60 seconds the building had disappeared, and the street was silent. It was the end not only for one of Atlanta's important structures, but a way of life for many who had been associated with the club. "I cried," admits Albert Happoldt. "That was a beautiful place. And it was home to us."

Buz McGriff waited until later in the week to drive by. He was stunned by the emptiness of the lot where the club had stood. "The building was gone, just wiped away. And the lot was cleared off, like somebody had cut the club off at ground level and moved it. The only sign it had been there was the muddy water where the pool had been. I knew it was more than just tearing down a building and moving to a new location. Our city was changing. That kind of lifestyle seemed to be gone."

The proud old structure had been overtaken by the demolition-and-replacement impetus that would characterize Atlanta in the seventies. *The Atlanta Constitution* captured both the significance and the irony of the event in a sentence: "The Atlanta Athletic Club at Carnegie Way and Cone Street, gathering place for Atlanta's socially prominent since the turn of the century, has been torn down and will be replaced with a 31-story, $28-million Treadway Inn hotel."

The events that led to the destruction of the Carnegie Way club were similar to the events that led to the sale of East Lake. Atlanta was changing, and that change flowed all around the club's facilities and through the lives of its members. The change that most affected the town club was the growth of the hotel and restaurant industry in downtown Atlanta. Downtown experienced a construction boom in the late 1960s and early 1970s; within the year before the destruction of the Carnegia Way club, 11 new hotels broke ground or announced plans. Among these were the Peachtree Plaza and the Atlanta Hilton. As the industry grew, the use of Carnegie Way's dining and overnight facilities declined markedly.

The city, prompted by the hotel and restaurant industry, also put pressure on clubs to give up the profitable civic club business. "We were very conscious of not competing with the private restaurants since we were nonprofit," says Glenn Dewberry, Jr., then president (later chairman) of Atlantic Steel and soon to succeed Eugene Branch as president of the Athletic Club. "Fifteen years before, we had had a lot of use from companies, but somehow or other it seemed to have slipped away from us. At lunchtime we were serving approximately 150 people, but that won't support a club with 40 rooms to rent."

Other factors compounded the problems of the downtown club. The widespread installation of air-conditioning plus the change to Daylight Savings Time reduced interest in the roof garden, which only cooled off when darkness fell. In addition, an increasing number of businesses built their own dining facilities. And, to compound the problem, Atlantans began to be wary of remaining downtown after dark.

The board stood by its downtown club. "We truly believe that the success of the Atlanta Athletic Club has to be based largely on a bigger and improved downtown facility," urged President Larry Martin at the annual stockholders' meeting on February 14, 1967. At the next year's meeting he confirmed this position. "I believe that we are not only committed to, but dependent on in the future, a strong downtown facility of the Athletic Club type. The central city is developing as the heart of a great metropolitan area. The Atlanta Athletic Club will be a short walk from the so-called 'Wall Street' of the South. As long as we have the correct suburban facilities, we can be a great downtown facility, attractive especially to young men who will be the top leaders of Atlanta in the future. We must keep these young men coming into our club."

In 1968 the board decided to redecorate the club with some $400,000 in funds from the sale of East Lake. The Fourth Floor Cocktail Lounge was renamed the Trophy Lounge and renovated in an attempt to broaden its appeal and absorb some of the business that had once gone to the roof garden (now closed). At the same time, AAC was proceeding with construction of a clubhouse and golf course at River Bend.

During this difficult time (in June 1965), M. M. "Chuck" Witherspoon, a graduate of Dartmouth College and former assistant manager of the New York Athletic Club, was hired as assistant general manager, ultimately to replace Clyde Mingledorff, who would retire in June 1969 after 26 and a half years with the club.

Despite these efforts, business did not improve at Carnegie Way. Only a few couples dined at night in the elaborate Crystal Room, and the 40 upstairs bedrooms held only 4 or 5 residents. The club found itself focusing on cost-cutting measures at Carnegie Way, such as replacing the elaborate breakfasts for residents with a coffee and roll setup. At this point the decision was painfully obvious to board members: the downtown club should be closed.

In retrospect, Martin, who served as president from 1965 to 1968, believes they should have moved sooner: "The whole board — I along with them — made an error in judgment. We thought that improvements and promotion downtown was what was needed. We failed to see that the center city was changing and our members just wouldn't patronize as before. We should have concentrated on River Bend earlier."

Still, it was a decision that lacked strong membership support for about two years. "Some members thought we should maintain it, but we were losing money, money, money," remembers Dewberry.

In 1971 the club made the decision to sell. "None of us had any crystal ball," says Eugene T. Branch, who was president of the club at the time, "but we knew we had to take drastic action if we were going to be a first-class club." In September, Branch announced that a buyer had been found — real estate developer George Griffeth. The price agreed upon was $1,030,000. Branch was quoted in the December 31, 1971, Atlanta Journal as saying, "Things are changing rapidly in our world —more rapidly than some of us may wish — and clubs have to respond to the changing desires of membership."

When the club closed on the last day of the year, Yolande Gwin carried these remarks in her column in The Atlanta Journal:

An Atlanta landmark will join with 1971 today, Friday, December 31, to become a part of history and sentimental memories.

Today, the last day of the year, will also be the last day the Atlanta Athletic Club [downtown] will be open. There will be no farewell party; no New Year's Eve party, no nothing in the way of farewell parties. After the lights blink out this evening there will be no more Atlanta Athletic Club in downtown Atlanta.

There is a country club, the Atlanta Athletic Club Country Club out near Norcross, and there is a Yacht Club at Lake Lanier, but these two are merely in swaddling clothes in a manner of speaking, as compared to the downtown club. . . . It is the downtown club which pulls at the heartstrings of thousands of Atlantans.

There was a final party at the club, after all — a small engagement party Branch and his wife held for their daughter Susan in the Crystal Room that night. It was the last time the famous chandeliers would grace the family celebrations of Atlanta Athletic Club members.

These chandeliers were the center of interest when the club's furnishings were auctioned off the following August. The set of three chandeliers had been imported from Czechoslovakia for $26,000 when the club was built in 1926. Eventually, the chandeliers took their place in the Dunwoody Baptist Church.

When the dust of the Carnegie Way club had settled, emotionally as well as physically, most remaining members agreed that selling had been the right decision. "The whole residential picture changed," sums up J. W. Jones. "In order to survive you had to go where the business was."

It was a painful period, in which friendships were broken and lives were changed, but gradually the members of both the Athletic Club and the East Lake club were reconciled to the events. Charlie Yates expressed the sentiment many came to feel in later years: "I am very proud of the fact that the East Lake golf course has been preserved and I'm also proud the Athletic Club decided they would move to the north part of Atlanta, where the real growth was. I am very proud of the judgment of the policymakers to realize that a move was necessary, given the changes in population pattern in Atlanta, and that they did decide to move out to the River Bend area."

History, however, left its own footnote of

irony. The site of the Carnegie Way club was not used, as planned, for hotel development. A decade after the club's destruction, the site was merely a parking lot. In addition, within a year of the club's closing, a group of young businessmen in Atlanta, not unlike the original founders of the Athletic Club, felt the need for an athletic facility downtown and formed the Downtown Athletic Club. Their location was 72 Edgewood Avenue, a few steps from the original location of the Atlanta Athletic Club.

It was a need the Atlanta Athletic Club could no longer serve. AAC was irretrievably committed to the families who had grown up in the club, celebrated their marriages in the club, and learned to love the game of golf. In the process they had become the club. And those families now lived primarily on the north side of the city.

Chapter Twelve

On the North Side

The newspaper description of the Athletic Club's northside facilities as being still "in swaddling clothes" was perhaps more appropriate than the writer realized. Even while the club was experiencing the loss of its East Lake and Carnegie Way facilities, rich in history and tradition, it was undergoing a rebirth on the north side of Atlanta. A rebirth that would lift the Athletic Club to its greatest recognition ever nationally and internationally. But for the time being, it had its work cut out for it in establishing itself on the north side.

Soon after the decision was made to sell the number two course in 1966, the club contracted with golf course architect Robert Trent Jones (unrelated to Bobby Jones) for the building of a 27-hole course on the northside property at a cost of $650,000. The three nines and an activity building (later to serve swimming and tennis) were ready for use by the 1967 season, giving Witherspoon four Athletic Club facilities to oversee — East Lake, Carnegie Way, Lanier Yacht Club, and River Bend Country Club (as the new facility was called). Club golf pro Harold Sargent began a 25-mile commute between the two country clubs, spending half a day at each.

A "name-the-nines" contest lent a spirit of fun to preparations for the May 27 opening. Out of 200 entries (many of them highly imaginative) the contest committee chose "Big Bend" for the nine with six dogleg holes, "Waterloo" for the nine with four lake holes plus the Chattahoochee River to contend with, and "Long View" for the nine that started with a long par 5. Some 700 members attended the opening, with President Larry Martin presiding at the ribbon-cutting and barbecue. Then 224 of them retrieved their clubs and initiated the new northside course with relish. The first foursome to tee off were Phil Denton, Robert Armstrong, Richard Whitehead, and Charlie Campbell.

Once the decision was made to sell East Lake (in the spring of 1968), the membership turned its attention more fully to its new golfing home,

Once the decision was made to sell the East Lake Club, the membership turned its attention to its new golfing home, which was being constructed at River Bend.

As the June 1970 opening date neared, the new clubhouse assumed its final form.

93

where an additional nine holes were being constructed (designed by Joe Finger). Since this was now the club's only golf facility, the board decided to rename the new club. The name "River Bend" had been adopted by too many other ventures in the area, and more important, this time the Athletic Club wanted its country club to bear the parent club's name. Too many people had failed to realize that East Lake belonged to the Atlanta Athletic Club. So in 1969 the club adopted a new name — the Atlanta Athletic Club Country Club.

Meanwhile, work was already under way on the clubhouse (designed by Sidney R. Barrett & Associates). The *Club Times* of November 1968 describes the plans:

> With a setting buried in a dense wooded pine thicket, the new Riverbend Country Club has been designed with a liberal use of wood and stone to reflect its natural surroundings. The Club building is made up of two major building elements, connected by a glass and wood frame promenade. One segment of the building contains all the facilities related to golf while the connecting segment furnishes all the necessary elements for the social aspects of the Club. While horizontal in form, the building mass is accented by two high roofed areas covered with rough cedar shakes.

> A feature of the golfing wing is the fact that it is a completely integrated golfing unit. The upper floor or entry level contains the men, ladies, and children's locker rooms plus the pro shop and starters platform. The lower level is made up of golf cart storage, bag room and indoor golf practice range. A golfer need not go outside the building to have access to all facilities.

> The all glass mixed grille and bar are located in the social wing which is elevated above the golf course and provides an excellent vantage point for all the starting tees and finishing greens. The mixed grille has a seating capability of approximately 250 people while the bar will hold 40 people.

On June 14, 1970, the membership celebrated the opening of its completed facilities — the clubhouse, Olympic-sized swimming pool, and five tennis courts. (The fourth nine opened late that summer as well.)

The closing of the Carnegie Way club in 1971 made the Country Club at River Bend and the Yacht Club at Lanier the only Athletic Club facilities.

Early Struggles

In spite of the jubilation over the new facilities, it was some time before members could rest easy with their decision to commit themselves entirely to the north side. The new clubhouse was a long way out from such areas as Buckhead and Ansley, and was even eight miles outside the perimeter highway being constructed around Atlanta. Demographic studies might show this to be the future growth corridor, but for the time being, it was a long and lonely drive. "It was out in the sticks," says John P. Imlay, Jr., who joined the club in 1966. "People thought we were crazy." Glenn Dewberry agrees, "We had gone from one extreme to another. We were way out in the country and it was difficult to get the facility used."

To compound the issue, although Witherspoon had remained with the club as general manager through these difficult changes, management at the River Bend club was constantly in transition. Mike Fraser helped to open the facility, but left soon after to go into private consulting. Don Mitchell managed the new club for about six months and was followed by George Lawlor. When it became apparent that the dining facilities were not patronized as they should be, the club hired James E. Petzing as director of food and beverages in June.

Since the growth of the 1930s, management of the Athletic Club's facilities had become increas-

Jim Petzing, general manager, built a strong management team for the club's new northside facilities.

ingly complex and the board had responded by hiring ever more experienced general managers. Happoldt had been hired almost directly out of college, but when he left the club in 1946, he was replaced by Mingledorff, who had served as auditor/secretary of the club for three years. Mingledorff was replaced by Chuck Witherspoon, who (as mentioned earlier) had been assistant manager of the New York Athletic Club. He had also worked for the BonAir Hotel in Augusta, the Atlanta Biltmore, and the Sapphire Valley Inn and Golf Club in North Carolina. Witherspoon served under Mingledorff for three years as operations manager and one year as joint manager before assuming full management in 1969. His successor was Jim Petzing.

Petzing came to the club with higher credentials than any of his predecessors. And he soon proved invaluable. Originally from Buffalo, New York, he had earned a degree at Cornell University in hotel, club, and restaurant management and had worked in food service for several years. With the house committee devising various approaches to get members to try the dining facilities, he soon built such a reputation for excellent food service at the club that lunch was filled to capacity almost every day and the club began to take reservations for the evening meal. "We had blue plate specials, bingo, and all kinds of things," remembers John Imlay, who headed the house committee at the time. "Paul Ebbs piped up at an annual meeting and said the martinis weren't big enough, so we installed a 13-ounce martini. We lost $18,000 that month, but we had the happiest members we've ever had! We also started a Casual Corner, where ties weren't required. People began to come, partly because we responded to their needs and partly because people were moving out that way."

The Yacht Club, meanwhile, continued to be a source of strength. These pioneers for AAC on the north side of town kept up the camaraderie they had been known for since the Yacht Club's beginning. By early 1970 the club was docking 52 houseboats, 10 sailboats, and 40 runabouts. And in July 1971 the *Club Times* reported: "At long last the lake and its surroundings begin to look like home. The water level is real good, foliage [is] on the trees and everywhere one looks, activity." The annual Pass in Review remained a highlight of the year, with a parade of craft all the way from sleek, tiny motorboats to ponderous houseboats. The colorful names included "Fellowship," "Pat Away," "Empty Pockets," "Heyward Hilton," "Yes Dear, Nod," "Lazy Evelyn," "DT's," "Family Affair," "Why Not," "Misbehaving," and "Miss Mini."

Another core group at AAC was the bowling league, which met faithfully in the early 1970s. It included such regulars as Jack and Iola Clardy, Bob and Mary Holman, Ruth and Gail Tomey, Rick and Katy Steinkamp, Mac and Sarah McLeod, Lou and Doris Sylvester, John and "DD" Cavanagh, Jim and Laura Castellaw, John and Joan Wiedeman, John and Virginia Law, Bill and Clara Gaik, Bill and Kay Jordan, Mike and Irene Perry, and Fred and Marie Bellinger.

When Lawlor resigned in October 1970, Jim Petzing was made manager of the country club, and when Witherspoon resigned in February 1971, Petzing became general manager for both clubs, a position he holds today. Management had stabilized, and membership support was beginning to rise.

A New Athletic Program

Under Jim Petzing's management, the new Athletic Club Country Club began to prosper. Development followed its expected northward path (an extension of Peachtree Industrial, a major artery from the club to the city, was opened in 1970), Atlanta continued to attract new businesses, Atlanta's newcomers continued to locate on the north side, and long-standing AAC members began to feel comfortable with their new home.

One of these was Bobby Jones, who had supported the move wholeheartedly. Jones believed the new course was of championship quality, and to prove it, he personally wrote to Robert K. Howse, president of the United States Golfing Association, on November 16, 1971, inviting the association to hold the U.S. Open at the Athletic Club.

> My home club, the Atlanta Athletic Club, has recently built a new country club consisting of two golf courses, each of eighteen holes, and the four nines being so designed that they permit consecutive play. The lay-out also embraces a spacious clubhouse and several ponds of some beauty.
>
> Although you will understand that I am not likely to take much part in a golf tournament in 1975, our membership is most eager to be awarded the privilege of entertaining the USGA Open Championship for that year; and I should be most happy if my old club should become the host for my favorite golf tournament.

When the association accepted the following year, selecting Atlanta as the site for the bicentennial year (1976), the board was reassured that its move to the north side promised a good future.

The remainder of the athletic program had not fared as well as golf. After having watched the (non-golfing) athletic program at Carnegie Way and East Lake dwindle, Buz McGriff considered leaving. He found himself with only a swimming and tennis program at River Bend and spent most of his time on maintenance and improvement projects for the golf courses. He kept his loyal athletes fit by arranging for the badminton players to play at the Northside YMCA and for the racquetball and handball players to play at the Jewish Community Center.

But the seed for a new and fundamentally different program had already been growing. It started with a physical fitness awareness across the entire country that was particularly visible in the Kennedy years. "Dr. Thomas K. Cureton, from the University of Illinois, had come to the downtown club to do a physical fitness clinic," says McGriff. That was the first flicker of the interest in running and in health. He talked about things that today seem commonplace, but then just weren't talked about — diet, smoking, alcohol, stress."

That fitness movement had grown by the time the club established itself at River Bend. In August 1968, the *Club Times* reported, "You're more likely to find bar bells than a bar in an executive suite these days. Business men are on a health kick and many are substituting regular exercise periods for their martini luncheons. . . . The trend is very definitely noticed here at the Athletic Club. There has been a sharp increase in physical activity within the last six months. More swimmers, more handball, badminton and weightlifting than ever before."

Even so, McGriff's fear was that AAC would not recognize the need for a strong non-golfing program. "The first building was the Aquatic Center," he says. "They had made up their minds they wanted swimming. Then it came to a decision: Are we going to build an athletic center?

He recalls the events that followed. "Richard Whitehead got up before the board and made an impassioned plea for an athletic program. He was backed up by Ed Stewart, Harry Cashin, and George Brodnax. The board sent out a survey to the members, but it did not come back as a mandate for a strong program. They decided to make a limited investment. In October 1973 the club opened its new athletic center, a freestanding building with a large gym for volleyball, basketball, and badminton; one squash and three racquetball courts; and exercise rooms equipped with five new weight machines called Nautilus machines. Larry Daniel "Dan" Thaxton was also hired as assistant athletic director.

McGriff was elated. "When we first opened, you could not get a racquetball court," he recalls. Handball also had a good following, led by such strong competitors as Bob Boylston and Tony Whatley. With the assistance of Dan Thaxton and Glenda "Bunny" Cook in gymnastics, McGriff began to build interest in the rest of the athletic program. "We were at the right place at the right time," he says. "All over the United States people were zeroing in on physical fitness. And now we had knowledge and tools to work with. We knew

Buz McGriff, longtime athletic director of the club, proudly demonstrated equipment at the opening of the new athletic center. (Seated is Mike Bolton.)

how fast to run and how far. We knew how much to lift." His enthusiasm was infectious, and the center began to attract a stronger following than board members had anticipated.

Tennis, meanwhile, was undergoing a nation-wide surge in popularity. A separate tennis facility had been opened at AAC in 1970 under the supervision of tennis professional Joe Becknell, with one hard-surface court, four green clay courts, and a pro shop. In 1971 Becknell was succeeded by Peter Howell, who saw a doubling of participation the next year, from 4,682 to 8,369. In 1973, with an average of 1,000 people a month participating in the tennis program, the board decided to build four additional courts, which were lighted for night play. And the following year it established a separate tennis committee, elevating tennis to the same status as golf and yachting in board representation.

The club's social facilities were also experiencing increased patronage, and it began to offer the nationally known entertainers it had offered at the city club, such as George Gobel and The New Christy Minstrels. To accommodate its gradually increasing membership, the club added a social

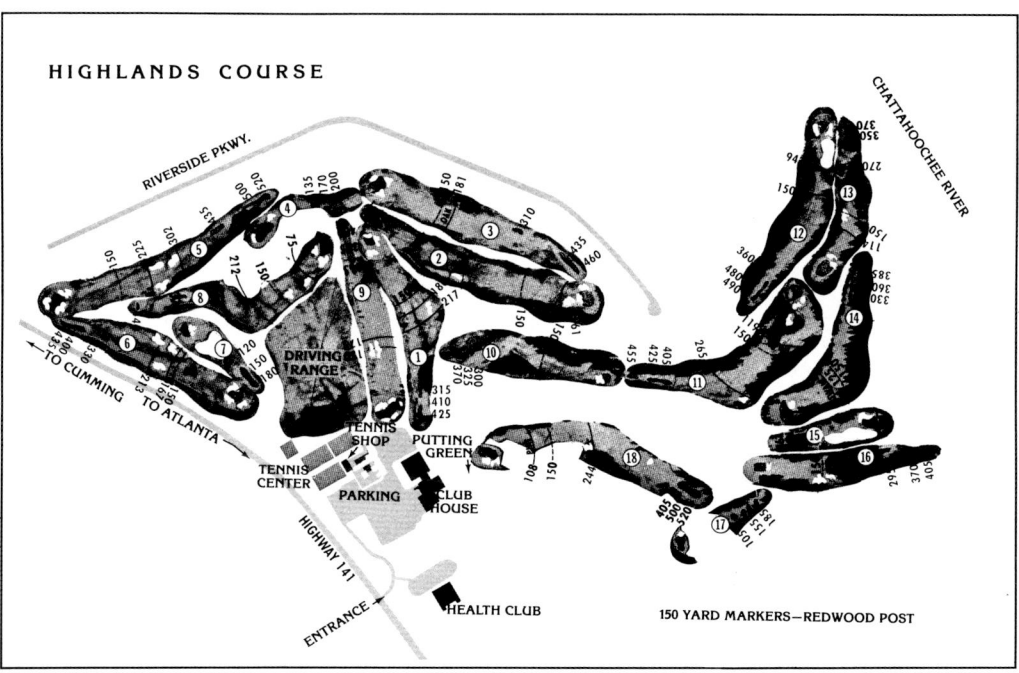

Both of the club's new courses proved to be championship courses. The U.S. Open was played on the Highlands course in 1976, and the U.S. Women's Open was scheduled for the Riverside Course in 1990.

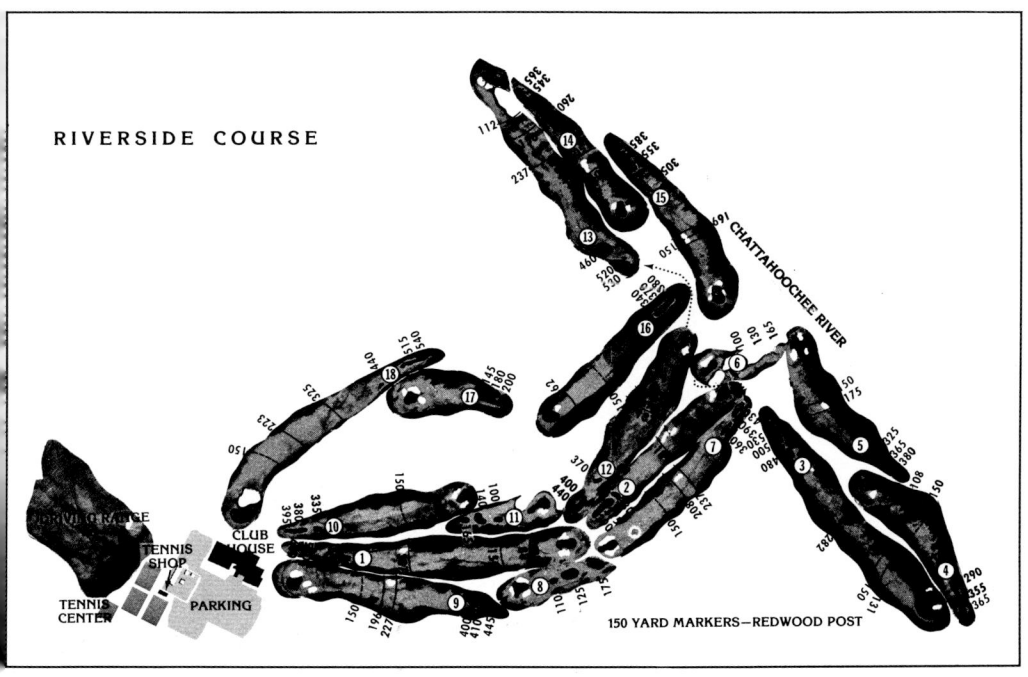

97

wing in 1973, naming the rooms after the courses Bobby Jones played in winning the 1930 Grand Slam — the Merion Dining Room, Interlachen Lounge, Hoylake Room, and St. Andrews Ballroom.

1973 had been a landmark year for the Athletic Club. Participation was significantly up, and for the first year since its move to the north side, the club had not run an operating loss.

An Era Passes

Bobby Jones' death in December 1971, a month after he wrote to Robert Howse, was a symbol to the older members than an era had passed. Gone were the caddies; now Jim Brett looked over the nines from a plate glass tower, directing starting tees. Gone were Bean's Boys and the competitive teams of the old days. And gone was the sense of intimacy. "Before, you knew everybody," reminisces Charlie Yates. "Old Dave was a locker man at East Lake so long. You could call Dave and he knew you by your voice. It's not as personalized now. I think that's true of any club in Atlanta."

Instead, a new sophistication was apparent with members of diverse backgrounds swept in by the Sunbelt phenomenon. And this new generation of members and their families identified the Atlanta Athletic Club with northside Atlanta.

The club had begun the difficult process of changing its image in Atlanta, but it did not want to lose touch with its past. The board resolved to build a special room to honor its most famous member and to communicate to the new generation of members some of the history of the club. It was to be ready for the upcoming U.S. Open.

Chapter Thirteen

Alligators, Walkie-Talkies, and Red Alerts

*O*n 1976 Bobby Jones' dream was realized: the 76th U.S. Open was held at the Atlanta Athletic Club on June 17-20 — the first time the Open had been held in the Southeast. The event marked a new era for the northside club in which it would not only become an established institution in Atlanta, but would also achieve national recognition.

Grown to 2,150 members, the club presented its visitors with prime facilities for the tournament. Its Highlands course, 7,015 yards long with a par 70, had undergone a $450,000 reconstruction under the supervision of golf architect George Fazio. All 18 greens had been reworked or rebuilt, every bunker had been changed, and some of the doglegs had been eliminated. Harold Sargent had remained within eye- and earshot of every change, nurturing "his" course for the big day. And the finished product had been immaculately groomed by Course Superintendent Bob McGee.

The restructured course gave the best golfers a run for their money. "Its awesome length, its Bermuda rough, the heat, the humidity, and the incumbent pressures of a major championship were combinations guaranteed to produce a worthy titleholder," wrote Larry Bush of the *Palm Beach Times* on the close of the first day's play.

The tournament was punctuated by a few testy complaints about the length of the grass, but spirits were generally high, especially among the members who participated in running the tournament. "I was on the security force," remembers John Imlay. "We were extremely careful about who was allowed where, especially on the terrace. I got this call, 'Red alert!' I said, 'What's the problem?' Somebody said, 'A snake has crawled up on the terrace.' " Imlay shot back, "Does it have a member badge on?" Asked if he had a disaster plan, Gene Branch, general chairman of the event, quipped, "What do you mean? With 14,000 automobiles and 30,000 people descending on us, the whole damn thing seems like an impending disaster."

But 1,200 AAC volunteers managed the tickets, parking, programs, gallery control, scoring, player and press accommodations, bleachers, food and beverages, and "ecology" (toilets) so well that visitors rated the club first-class. Furman Bisher, writing for *The Atlanta Constitution* on June 20, the final day of the tournament, captured the flavor of the event:

> . . . I knew it was the U.S. Open when —
>
> An amateur still not out of college shot the course down in cold blood the first day and not a pro could break par.
>
> The same amateur, realizing what he had done, that this is war not just fun, could not break 80 the second round. . . .
>
> Hale Irwin complained about the grass on the fairways and a task force of USGA admirals flew into the breach, nervelessly taking command and putting back into place with 3,000 words an infant crisis that could have been handled in 20. . . .
>
> The amateur who shot 67 on Thursday says, perplexedly, 'You mean there was something wrong with the grass?' . . .
>
> The press bus got lost trying to find the way from the motel to the course. . . .
>
> A kid barely 18 and barely out of high school showed up with his best pal as his caddy. . . .
>
> John A. Gentile, Wayne Levi and Calvin Peete made the cut but Bill Casper didn't. Not to mention Bruce Crampton, Frank Beard, Bobby Nichols, Tom Kite and a whole host of others, as they say of tacklers.
>
> The 18th hole was enthusiastically heralded as 'one of the great finishing holes of golf.'

As Bisher indicates, human nature kept the tournament full of surprises. But the volunteers had clearly brought it off; the Athletic Club had done a creditable job of managing one of the major golf tournaments in the world.

With a record crowd of 29,507 spectators to watch him, Jerry Pate of Pensacola, Florida, won

For the 1976 Open the U.S. Post Office authorized a special temporary branch, named after one of Bobby Jones' golf clubs.

the Open with a birdie on the final hole, giving him a two-under-par 68 for the last day, 277 for the tournament (three under par), and a check for $42,000. He had beaten Al Geiberger and Tom Weiskopf by a two-shot margin. His fourth-round 194-yard, five-iron shot over the lake on the 18th hole that day would be selected three years later as one of the greatest shots in history by *Golf Magazine.*

After the tournament was over, P. J. Boatwright, Jr., executive director of the USGA, gave AAC's membership a well-deserved accolade in a letter of July 2, 1976. "We hope that the Atlanta Athletic Club will see fit to invite the USGA to have the Open, as well as other USGA events, at your marvelous facility in the future. . . . With a few more minor changes in the course, it could, in my opinion, be ranked as one of the 10 best courses in the country."

It was a grand moment for a club that had struggled to reestablish its identity — not as the "City Club" or "East Lake Country Club," but as the Atlanta Athletic Club. Wrote Gene Branch proudly in the August *Club Times,* "We've earned the right to forever look out at the 18th green, remember what it looked like late in the evening of June 20 at the finish of the 1976 Open, and say to ourselves: 'Man, we really put on one hell of a show.' "

Another dream was realized as well that summer. The Robert T. Jones, Jr., Memorial Room was opened in time for the tournament, with all four of Jones' Grand Slam trophies on display and the heads of the world's greatest golfing associations on hand for the ceremony. Pictures of Jones from the age of 6, when he won his first neighborhood golf tournament, to the age of 28, when he won the Grand Slam of golf, told the remarkable story of an individual athlete's achievements.

The room also told the story of a remarkable club. A trophy given to Jones by the club in 1916 and inscribed "our own little Bob" indicated the kind of support the club offered its young athletes. And the pictures and trophies of Alexa Stirling Fraser, Watts Gunn, and Charlie Yates showed that Jones was not the only outstanding golfer the club had nurtured. Displayed were the two golf balls used by Jones and Gunn in the 1925 U.S. Amateur, the only time two players from the same club had met in the finals. This was a remarkable group of athletes, produced by the special combination of native talent, excellent facilities, superior instruction, strong competition, and an environment of stimulation and encouragement. The Athletic Club had succeeded in communicating to people all over the world and to its own new generation of members part of the history that made this, in anybody's book, a special club.

The Robert T. Jones, Jr. exhibit which was in the National Portrait Gallery, Smithsonian Institution, 1981—1982.

Alexa Stirling cut the ribbon to open the Robert T. Jones, Jr., Memorial Room. L — R: Harold Sargent, Robert T. Jones, IV, Watts Gunn, and Charlie Yates.

An Established Institution

The new Athletic Club facility took on the aura of an established institution in the next decade. By April 1980, membership use of the club was "robust," in the words of President Graydon Hall and only 100 vacancies remained; by April 1981 Merriell Autrey, Jr., who had assumed the presidency after Hall, reported the club had reached capacity, with a membership of 2,416.

Part of the new aura of success came from the repeated selection of AAC as host for national and international golfing events. "One of our objectives was to make the club more visible and, I guess, more prestigious," says Don W. Sands, who had joined the board in 1978. "To do that, we had to get some more tournaments." The next big AAC tournament was the 1981 PGA Championship, held August 3-9.

The event meant a lot of hard work for volunteers and for Course Superintendent Jim Ganley, who had replaced Bob McGee in January 1980. But the horseplay quotient guaranteed the work wouldn't be a chore. "It's held in August each year, which is not a good month. That's sort of dog days in golf, like it is in baseball. It's hard to get press," explains Neal Purcell, who served on the steering committee. "We were planning this one about the time Jerry Pate won the Memphis Classic. Right after he won, he dove into the lake on the eighteenth hole, and John Imlay's idea was to put a fake alligator in the lake with a sign, 'Come on down, Jerry!' It's one of the few times John lost a vote on the committee."

The crowds came anyway, alligator or not, and so did bad weather. As lightning crackled over the course, Bill (W. W.) Gaston, general chairman of the event (and past president of the club), marshalled his troops to cope with the situation. "You could tell he enjoyed it," recalls Purcell. "He got on the walkie-talkie to call in the steering committee. And sure enough we had one or two people come into the crisis center. It was tough. He was the right man at the right time for that tournament."

Larry Nelson, a golfer who was born near the new AAC location and represented Pine Tree Country Club in Kennesaw, won the tournament. Nelson was something of an anomaly because he started playing golf when he was 21. "It definitely was no fluke," however, cautioned Jim Warters in the September 1981 issue of *PGA Magazine.* He continued:

He was 7-under-par 273 for four rounds over a demanding Atlanta Athletic Club Highlands Course made even more difficult by rough so deep and thick that balls landing within a few feet of officials often required several minutes to locate.

The still slender Nelson, now with thinning hair, won by four shots over 1979 Masters champion Frank Urban (Fuzzy) Zoeller. And he was never seriously threatened by anyone after a birdie run that netted him his second straight 66 on Saturday. 70-66-66-71-273. That was the mathematical account of Nelson's triumph over the same course where Jerry Pate won the 1976 U.S. Open with a 277 total.

Larry Nelson, an Atlantan, won the 1981 PGA Championship, the second major tournament held at the new northside facility.

But the story goes beyond pure mathematics. With an all-professional field, this was the strongest array of major championship contenders in the world, including defending champion Jack Nicklaus and such international stars as Severiano Ballesteros, Sandy Lyle, Isao Aoki, Gary Player and Greg Norman.

For his fine performance, Nelson took home a purse of $60,000. The Athletic Club again set records for attendance and revenues and took home a growing reputation as a first-class club with a tough championship course.

On September 21-25, 1982, the club hosted another big golfing event — the Commercial Union Junior World Cup Tournament, the premier international junior golf competition, which pits the two top juniors from each of 16 countries against each other in match and medal play. For the 1982 tournament, AAC families volunteered to serve as hosts for the 32 participating boys, and General Chairman Charles Brown became the control center for an unusual, family-oriented event. Although

the U.S. team were the defending winners, Spain came out victorious. The gallery was disappointed, but interest in junior golf was heightened. And a broader group of golfers came to appreciate the Atlanta Athletic Club.

Strength in Athletic Programs

The continued success of its own athletic programs also contributed to the recognition of AAC as an established institution. AAC golfers, for example, were performing at top levels in state, regional, and national competitions. Charles Harrison, who had won the Southern Amateur Championship in 1955 and the Georgia State Amateur Championship in 1959 continued to be a prime contender in national and international competitions. In 1972 he was fifth in the U.S.G.A. National Amateur Medal Play, and in 1980 he was a quarter-finalist in the British Amateur. Tom Forkner gained his first successes by winning the Georgia Seniors Championship in 1968 and 1969. By 1974 he was

Martha Wilkinson Kirouac became the U.S. Women's Amateur Champion in 1972.

Larry Nelson (pictured with his wife) took home a purse of $60,000; the AAC took home a growing reputation as a first-class club with a tough championship course.

ranked among the top 10 amateurs in the United States, with wins in the International Seniors Championship and The Breakers International Invitational Championship. During the 1970s he competed regularly in the U.S.G.A. Seniors Amateur and took the Western Seniors Championship in 1978, 1980, and 1983. Martha Wilkinson Kirouac became the U.S. Women's Amateur Champion in 1972. And Buck Hightower began to collect Southern senior wins in the 1970s. In 1976 he won the International Seniors Championship in Clearwater, Florida, and in 1979 the American Seniors Championship.

As it had in the past, the AAC golfing staff provided the support and encouragement needed for developing fine golfers. When Harold Sargent re-

tired as pro in 1978, he was succeeded by his brother Jack. "Jack was a unique person in that he was a student of golf rules," comments Imlay, who became president of the club in 1982. "While other people would read a novel, he'd read the rule book. When we went to the Pro-President tournament, people would gather around to ask his opinion. At one of these tournaments there was a heavy rain the night before. The officials told us that in the trap, where there was water, you could roll the ball over

and get a good lie. He refused to do it. It was against the rules. He was mad about it."

As a result of his expertise on rules, Jack Sargent became one of the rulesmen at the PGA, Masters, and TPC championships. "He was a great asset as an ambassador for the club," comments Imlay.

In 1980 two events occurred to remind the club of its golfing heritage. The club celebrated the 50th anniversary of Bob Jones' Grand Slam by sponsoring a Grand Slam Tour of the sites of his 1930 victories. And Charlie Yates received the Bob Jones Award from the United States Golf Association in recognition of his distinguished sportsmanship in golf. As members took pleasure in remembering the victories of these two top golfers, they were confident that the club would continue to produce international-quality competitors.

At the tennis center, champions had not yet clearly developed. But the tennis program was demonstrating a strength few would have anticipated a decade before. Club competitions were being held for all age groups and attracted outside players. In addition, an Annual Men's Member-Guest Tournament was held every June, and an Annual Professional Invitational and Pro Am was held in July or August. Frequently in the winner's circle were Hill Griffin and Steve Davis, both former college players who had won a number of Southern tennis championships.

The young players who were growing up on AAC courts (much as Bobby Jones and Alexa Stirling had grown up on East Lake's golf course) were also showing promise. In 1978 the *Club Times* conjectured, "Somewhere out there in the Atlanta Athletic Club is a potential Chris Evert...." It turned out to be no idle claim. The next year twin 8-year-old sisters, Shannan and Shawn McCarthy, began to play competitively. Three years later, in 1982, both girls were nationally ranked and moving up fast.

At the Athletic Center the emphasis was less on champions than on broad, enthusiastic participation. Attendance at the center surged as members began to use the Nautilus equipment and as running began to take hold. From 19,000 member visits in 1974 it grew to 30,663 in 1980 and 40,946 in 1982. McGriff's program was a ringing success.

As a symbol of the club's new emphasis on non-golfing athletics, in 1976 McGriff created an annual Sports Appreciation Night that honors an outstanding U.S. athlete. John Imlay presented the first "Atlanta Athletic Club Trophy" to Fran Tarkenton. (Others who have since received the award include Jerry Pate, Ted Turner, Leeman Bennett, Harold Sargent, Hubie Brown, William Andrews, Bill Curry, Steve Lundquist, Steve Bartkowski, George Rogers, Erskine Russell, Larry Nelson, R. L. "Bobby" Dodd, Dan Magill, Dale Murphy, Bobby Pate, Joe Torre, Pat Dye, A. J. "Duck" Swann, Bobby Cremins, Bo Jackson, Hugh Durham, Jeff Van Note, and Mike Fratello.) In 1979 another highly popular annual event was launched: the 10-kilometer run. A committee of members including Don Hall, Lewis Reeves, Joe Finley, and Guy Crain) planned the event as an invitational that included members from other clubs in metropolitan Atlanta. Mark Thompson of Druid Hills Golf Club took home first place honors with a time of 33:37, a record that stands to this day.

In badminton, the club received long-deserved recognition when it hosted the Southern Badminton Tournament in March 1979. The March *Club Times* reminded members, "When this elite tournament was in its infancy, the AAC provided the backbone for the organization. Cam Mitchell, Ed Patton, Guy Johnson, Bill Braswell, Jim Carlton, Bill Rocker, Allen McGhee, and Jim Taylor were

among the members who dominated play for years at the downtown club." The next year Guy Johnson (whose son Robert had also become an outstanding player) was elected president of the Southern Badminton Association. And in 1985, at his suggestion, AAC hosted the United States Badminton Association Championship.

In racquetball the club also hosted a national event. In 1984 the club picked up on a proposal by member Dick Andrews and sponsored a National Senior Racquetball Tournament that raised $20,000 for leukemia research at Emory University. Lewis Reeves, Neil Christman, and Duane Hoover pitched in to make the event successful.

The club even found a way to get its youth back on the basketball court. Working with Neal Purcell, Charlie Brown, and Connor Nelson, the athletic department invited Coach Bobby Cremins and his Georgia Tech "Yellow Jackets" to the club in 1982 for a basketball clinic, an event that would also become annual.

Though members were highly active in planning these events, McGriff was given much of the credit for the athletic program's success. He became a symbol for the entire club's pride in its athletic accomplishments at the northside facility. " 'Coach' Buz McGriff has stimulated interest

Bob Bell, longtime employee at the Yacht Club, received his 20-year pin in 1982.

105

among members of all ages," wrote the *Club Times* in May 1980. "Junior programs at the Club are perhaps the finest in the southeast. Swimming, gymnastics, aerobics, jogging, and racquet sports are constantly in demand for today's athletes. Both Club and Inter-Club Tournaments are extremely competitive and filled with enthusiasm. Programs offered at the Atlanta Athletic Club have increased so dramatically that the demands warranted two assistants for Buz. Together, they have [exemplified] the winning combination of physical fitness and fun." In 1982 McGriff was one of two AAC staffers to receive 20-year pins awarded by the club. (The other recipient was Bob Bell.) At the annual meeting President John Imlay said simply, "Buz exemplifies the spirit of the Atlanta Athletic Club."

Meanwhile, at the Yacht Club the addition of a deck around the clubhouse fostered a resurgence in participation. According to Jack R. Kelly, Jr., who would become commodore in 1984, "The old clubhouse was dark and drab, just not a place for people to meet and socialize. When the deck was added a little miracle happened. People started gathering up there." Regulars in the late 1970s and early 1980s included Peter and Pat Giles, Johnny and Lane Mitchell, Ron and Lola Harding, Paul and Jean Ebbs, Tom and Linda Cantrell, Jack and Pat Kelly, Larry and Renee Garrett, and Howard and Barbara Moore.

With increased participation, the Yacht Club added to what was already an ingenious array of regular parties. In August 1982, the club held its first Mystery Island Party, which requires boaters to follow a map to find their way to the party site. The slate of events also included Bob's Bull Roast, a Leaf Cruise to the north Georgia mountains, a Shipwreck party, a January Deep Freeze party, a Cast-Off party, a Progressive Dock Party in midsummer, and the long-standing Pass in Review. The Yacht Club program, like the club's other programs, had developed both the size and the traditions to assure a stable future.

Jim Petzing had provided the management continuity that allowed all of the club's programs to grow and prosper. A nationally recognized professional in his field, he was often a guest lecturer at the Florida State University School of Hotel and Restaurant Administration and the Cornell University School of Hotel Administration. He had also become active in the *Chaines des Rostisseurs*. His professionalism was apparent in the success of AAC's operations. "At a point when the budget reaches a certain size, a general management role is needed," says Imlay. "Jim brought together the general management concept. With Chris Borders [who joined as assistant manager in 1975 and soon became manager] and Chef Kurt Eisele, he developed a management team that rivals that of a great corporation." (In recognition of this achievement, Petzing would be elected president of the Club Managers Association of America in 1986.)

Investing in the Future

The events and victories of the early 1980s kept interest in the Athletic Club high. Its membership roster was consistently full, and the club had a waiting list to boot. Club events were often sold-out affairs. When the club held its first annual champagne picnic under the stars with the Atlanta 'Pops' Orchestra in 1983, it was sold out the first year. The club was confident enough of its success to make major investments in its facilities.

The first was an indoor tennis center, complete with four indoor courts, a pro shop, locker facilities, and lounge. The club opened the facility on July 12, 1983, four years after the arrival of Charles C. Benedict, III, as tennis professional to replace Peter Howell. Benedict came to AAC from the Louisville Country Club, where he had been director of tennis. "When I interviewed in 1979 the program was low in interest among members, and one of the questions posed to me was did I think the club should have indoor tennis," remembers Benedict. "I said they did if they wanted to be a premier club. Four years after that they did it. Now the tennis facilities are second to none. There are clubs that have more indoor courts, clubs that have more outdoor courts. But we have the mix. We're not the largest tennis center in the city, but we're equal to any club."

With the indoor center came a second rise in interest in tennis. And the club soon had a full complement of teams to compete in the Atlanta Lawn Tennis Association (ALTA), a city-wide competition involving some 45,000 people. "ALTA keeps the Atlanta tennis market a unique situation," says Benedict. "That's why an Atlanta club can't exist just as a golf club."

The board also decided on a major upgrading of the clubhouse facilities, financed by the sale of 100 acres of unused property across the highway. "The clubhouse had been up for about 12 years. It was modern and open in style, with a cavernous hall straight out to the golf course, and as it aged, it didn't look really first-class," explains Imlay. The board also felt the need for formal dining facilities. The original dining facilities in the Merion Room had been informal, since the Carnegie Way club, with its formal dining rooms, had existed when it was built. With the town club gone, AAC decided to make the social wing an elegant area, with a handsome dining room and a large ballroom. Ferry-Hayes was selected as the design firm for the project.

Neal Purcell, who chaired the effort, counts the renovation as one of his proudest contributions. In the words of fellow board member Don Sands, who would become president in 1984, "A club like AAC is made up of a lot of entrepreneurs, leaders in business and the city, and they all want high quality. They not only have worked hard at business and community; they've worked hard at the social side of life. It's people who aren't necessarily old Atlanta. They've worked their way up. They're achievers. They want the club to be an achiever." But Purcell faced a challenge because some of the long-standing members were skeptical of the need for the elaborate upgrading.

The grumbling died away as the project moved forward. Purcell recounts the changes: "We transformed a 'bowling alley' into a beautiful walkway to the golf pro shop and created a president's gallery in the process. We moved the Bobby Jones room to give it more prominence and, in the process, gained security. And we made major changes in the dining area. We split the grill into a bar, a luncheon room more conducive to family dining, and a sitting room. The most significant change was in the dining room; we created loggia dining, an informal dining atmosphere in a formal dining area — it's almost like being in a separate room. And we changed the lighting and decor to make the main dining room very formal."

The process took almost two years. In the early stages Purcell took his family to the grill for dinner one night and faced a barrage of complaints. "My wife said, 'Is it worth it?' I had my doubts at that time." As each area was completed, however, the renovation gained acceptance, especially since no assessment was involved. By the time of the grand opening on September 29, 1983, the club was wholeheartedly celebrating the changes that gave it the first elegant dining facilities since the closing of the downtown club in 1971. Says Purcell, "We took a facility that had no character and gave it character. It lacked pizazz. Ferry-Hayes added that." His moment of greatest satisfaction came at the annual meeting the following February, when "one of the members who had blasted it right from the start hobbled up and said, 'I want you to know the renovation was worth it. It's a magnificent project.' "

With its facilities refurbished, the club was pleased to host, on September 29-October 4, 1984, the U.S.G.A. Mid-Amateur Championship, a relatively new event created for golfers 25 years and older who remain amateurs and pursue the game as an avocation. Neal Purcell, who would become president in 1986, was general chairman.

Bouyed by the club's record of tournament successes and by the anecdotes of good times behind the scenes, the members readily volunteered for the preparations.

The process began in August 1983. Purcell met with his 9-person steering committee and many of

Neal Purcell and Bill O'Callaghan flank the winner of the 1984 Mid-Amateur Championship, Mike Podolak.

the 150 to 200 volunteers at least once a month right up until tournament time. "We had 31 people in leadership positions who were invited to a 7:30 meeting on a Saturday morning," he recalls. "All 31 showed up. That shows you what cooperation we have."

The November *Club Times* described the event:

The format called for 36 holes of medal play with the 64 players [out of 150] having the lowest scores advancing to match play competition. One of the tournament's exciting moments involved a 15 way playoff for the final seven spots in the match play portion of the tournament. Seven Georgians advanced to the match play portion of the competition. They were Danny Yates, co-medalist of the medal play qualifying with a score of 146, Seth Knight, Walter Driver, Robert Young, all from Atlanta, and William Ploeger of Columbus, Alan Doyle of La Grange and William Holbrook of Rome. Yates, Driver, Young, and Holbrook won first round matches and Young advanced to the quarterfinals before being eliminated.

The winner was something of a dark horse. He was

Michael Podolak, a 31-year-old insurance executive from Fargo, North Dakota, who barely qualified for match play competition with a score of 157, one point below the cut of 158. He had tried to qualify for the match play portion of the tournament since it began, but had never done so before. "He was a pleasant and outgoing fellow," remembers Purcell. "He was just pleased to be there, much less to win." The crowds were also apparent- ly glad to be there; again AAC broke tournament records for attendance.

This time the club was not surprised, and neither were the visitors. Through the 1976 U.S. Open, the 1981 PGA Championship, and the 1982 Junior World Cup, this club had come to be recognized as one of the top facilities for golf in the United States. And, unlike in the days of Bobby Jones' victories, the club was now clearly known as the Atlanta Athletic Club.

Eugene T. Branch, J. Neal Purcell, John P. Imlay, Jr., F. M. Bird and Larry H. Garrett cut the ribbon at the dedication for the remodeled clubhouse.

Chapter Fourteen

The Past and the Future

"Although we have no sure formula for judging the future, I would like to make my own prediction that the Club will be even greater. . . . I can say this because I believe the minds of men are capable of anything . . . through our legacy everything is in them . . . all the past as well as the future."

— Harry L. Cashin

In the spring of 1986 one of Neal Purcell's first official acts as president of the club was to dedicate the Royal Troon Room to Charlie Yates, who had won the British Amateur at the Royal Troon Golf Club in Ayshire, Scotland, in 1938. John Imlay emceed, caddies from the Augusta National club sang spirituals, and Charlie Yates returned the compliment by crooning a Scottish folk ballad to the crowd of 300. It was a night of high spirits, a time for looking back on the club's history, and a time for looking forward.

Looking Back

In hindsight, the club's pivotal decision in 1968 to commit to the north side of Atlanta was the right decision. It put the club in what had become the highest-growth area for golf in the United States. Within a six-mile radius of the club, four other clubs had opened courses or were in the process of doing so: the Country Club of the South (a community on 786 acres, with Jack Nicklaus as its spokesman), the Atlanta National, the Standard Club, and St. Ives Country Club. The long-predicted demographic spillover to the north side of Atlanta had actually come to pass, and the Athletic Club had been in the vanguard. "The club had to move away from its membership for awhile," observes Don Sands. "Now the membership is moving toward the club."

In the process of moving and reestablishing it-self, the club had changed, as it had at several points in its history. In 1908 it had embraced golf and country club living when it opened East Lake. In the 1920s it had broadened its athletic program to include families and to place more emphasis on individual sports. In 1970 it had lost the continuity of several member families when it moved to River Bend. And now the diversity of its new members had given the club a slightly different character.

But it had not become, as many had feared when it moved to River Bend, "just another run-of-the-mill athletic club." As host to one spectacular international event after another, it had gradually reclaimed the luster and excitement it had during the time of Bobby Jones and his well-loved father, Colonel Jones.

It had also recaptured many of the values that had made it an outstanding club in its earliest years. Buz McGriff points to the decision to build the Athletic Center. "People have said to me, 'What if

Charlie Yates does the honors at the dedication of the Royal Troon Room in 1986. L — R: Don Sands, John Imlay, Mrs. Charles R. Yates.

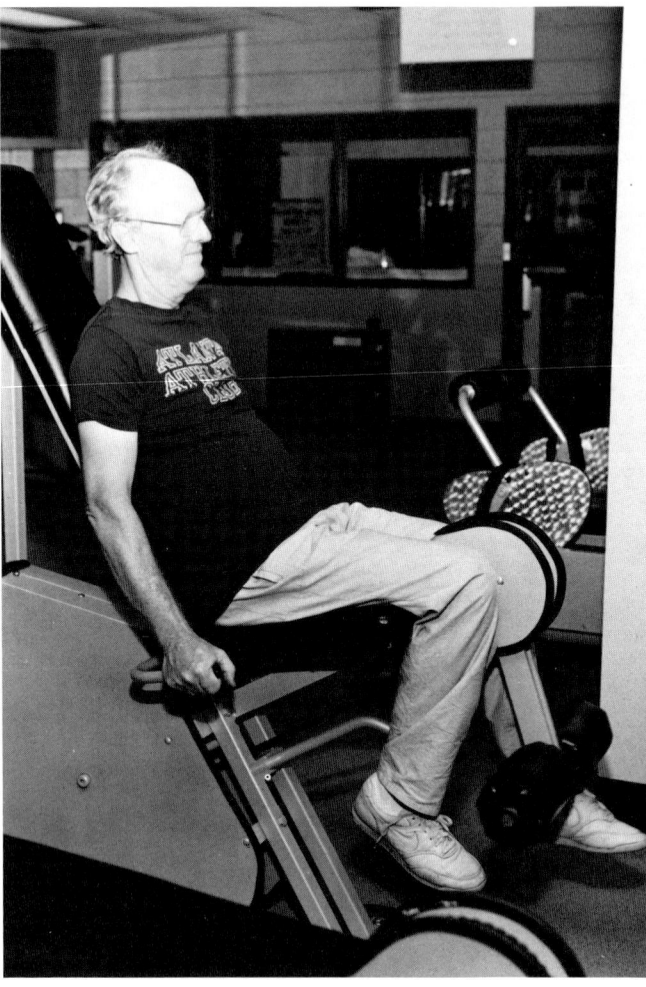

Jack DeLay

the board had decided not to build the center?' That was a turning point in the club's history." In fact, it was a return to the values of earlier times. Sports of all kinds were again a strong part of AAC, as they had been when the club was started on Edgewood and before East Lake Country Club was opened. "The major concern in the East Lake days was the golf courses. Times have changed now," acknowledges Hugh Wilson, an avid golfer who joined the club in 1931. "We still have the golf courses, but the club is much more a family establishment now. There's much more activity with the health club and the tennis courts and all of that. It's a much more varied, personal approach than in those days."

The club once again revolved around businessmen and their families, as it did when it was founded nearly a century ago. And it offered those families a broad mix of athletic and social activities. "It wasn't organized to be a great golf club or a great tennis club. It was organized to be a good place to meet socially and encourage members to exercise," says Don Sands. "That tradition has continued. I don't believe there's any club in the city that has the diversity of facilities for exercise."

The Future

What does the future hold? Probably not high growth, either in membership or facilities. AAC has reached a plateau, at least for the time being. "It's my personal opinion that the club is as big as it ever needs to get," adds Sands. "And I think we have all the facilities in place that a club needs. You'll see refinements to the facilities. Hopefully we'll keep it fresh and vital, instead of letting it get old and stodgy."

The excitement of the future will be in further recognition and achievement. In the fall of 1986 the United States Golf Association announced the selection of AAC to host the U.S. Women's Open in 1990. Observes Sands, "We've had the two great men's pro tournaments outside the Masters; we've had the U.S. Women's Amateur, and now we're gonna have the U.S. Women's Open. It kind of rounds out our activities." For the first time, too, the officials had chosen not the Highlands course for the play, but the Riverside course. "People think we've got one good championship course. We've got two good championship courses," boasts Sands, "and everyone will know about it when the Women's Open is played."

There is also the promise of more national and international champions in golf and tennis. The golfing program continues to be strong. Jack Sargent died of a heart attack on January 8, 1985,

"We still have the golf courses," says Hugh Wilson, "but the club is much more a family establishment now."

Mr. & Mrs. Tom Fowler

Bill Bryant, Sr.

"Bubba" Tindol

Bill, Cynthia, and Jessica Porter

111

L — R: Marion & John Mills, Pete & Jan McElroy

Patsy Cusick

Ryan Engle wins 1st place in Halloween Pumpkin carving contest.

L — R: W. H. Sibley, Alfred A. Wickliffe, John Wiedeman

112

ending 53 years of association of the Sargent family with AAC. He was replaced by Jack Weston Lewis, Jr., a graduate of Wake Forest University in Winston-Salem, North Carolina, who joined the AAC staff on May 27, 1985. Lewis brought to the Club an outstanding record as an amateur and professional golfer. He was a member of the 1967 Walker Cup Team (the youngest member at 19) and the 1968 U.S. World Amateur Team (as the second-ranked amateur in the United States); in 1968 he went on to win the North-South Amateur Championship. He turned pro in 1969, repeatedly won the North Carolina Open, and was a member of the 1980 U.S. PGA Team. He came to AAC from the Forsyth Country Club in Winston-Salem, North Carolina, where he was head golf professional.

Lewis has continued to participate in state and national competitions. "He's a real competitor," says Purcell. "He'll do something significant in golf. I would not be surprised to see him win the Georgia Open." The only surprise for members comes when Lewis does *not* perform well. Purcell fondly tells of a trip to the 1985 PGA Championship tournament at Cherry Hills in Colorado: "Jack had a good par on the first hole, but when he got to the next hole he two-putted from two feet. It was worth the trip to see him do that! We had eye contact until then; I don't think he looked at me after that."

Lewis would like to see AAC produce another generation of national-level competitors. With that goal in mind he sponsored a summer program for junior golfers in 1985 and 1986 that included clinics and a junior championship. He now plans to expand that into a year-round program.

Meanwhile, AAC's senior golfers continue to capture national trophies. In April 1986 Buck Hightower won the American Match Play Championship, a remarkable victory at 69 years of age. The next month Tom Forkner won the Western Seniors Championship. The *Club Times* reported in July 1986:

> Irony does play its part between these two gentlemen. Not only have they played golf competitively for 20 years at the Atlanta Athletic Club and at country clubs throughout the United States, their personal championship titles have been nearly equal. Tom and Buck boast the fact that within 80 rounds of golf played in one year, they remain only $10.00 apart in total winnings.

The club's junior golfers will clearly have role models for years to come.

The indications are already there that tennis champions may be evolving. Charles Benedict

Bill O'Callaghan, Bob Lester, Tom Forkner

Terry Traynor & Tom Blaska

113

Mr. & Mrs. E.B. Davis

Mr. & Mrs. George Miles

L — R: Len Hoshall & Mike Samford

Chris Lane & Jennifer Smith

Jeff & Scott Brown & Dan Mullins

Larry Garrett, Don Sands, John Wells, Gene Meason

115

started a junior tennis program when he arrived in 1979, and today the results are apparent. In September 1985 the club sent its first "graduate" to college on a tennis scholarship: Laurie Jackson, who entered Wake Forest University. And the club's promising twin players, Shannan and Shawn McCarthy, 16 years old in 1986, have generated some real excitement. In 1986 they were ranked among the top 15 players nationally, and the McCarthy family was named Family of the Year by the Southern Tennis Association. In November 1986 Shannon capped off the year by winning the doubles title in the National Indoor Junior Championship (partnered with Amy Frazier from Michigan). Many members are now comparing her to Bitsy Grant, the AAC member who led the club's early, highly spectacular tennis achievements.

Benedict is justifiably pleased. "There's no doubt golf has been the major strength of the club, but we around the tennis center are setting our mark now. These junior players are competing on a national level, and when people hear about the Atlanta Athletic Club now, it's often through tennis." Neal Purcell agrees, "We've reverted back to the early 1900s in tennis — back when we were a powerhouse. I think the club will have major champions in the next decade — at least at the state level if not at the national level."

If any champions do develop, they will have all the backing they need from AAC, a club that has always loved champions, particularly those who grew up on its grounds. If not, the club will continue to offer its greens and courts to future champions from other places. And take enormous pleasure in watching young men and women stretch for a goal that may seem unattainable. "It's been said that AAC could have another "A" in its name because of our interest in amateur sports," jokes Purcell. "We're probably one of, if not the only club to host a major tournament in each of the last five decades: in 1950, the U.S. Women's Amateur; in 1963 the Ryder Cup; in 1976, the U.S. Men's Open; in 1981 the PGA Championship; in 1982 the Junior World Cup; in 1984 the U.S. Mid-Amateur; and now in 1990, the U.S. Women's Open."

To the members, these tournaments, held at their club on the north side of Atlanta, were recognition of what they had fought to prove since their break with the old clubs at East Lake and Carnegie Way — this was no ordinary club. It was determined to be part of the future, but it would continue to demonstrate and thrive on the heritage of a remarkable past.

* * *

The swell buckboards of Burton Smith's day had given way to the T-models of George Adair's

The new golf courses on the north side proved to be championship quality.

116

time. The lean times of Scott Hudson's presidency had given way to the growth years of Colonel Jones. The grand old buildings downtown had given way to new hotels and office buildings. Atlanta was no longer a high-spirited country town bent on becoming a city. It was a full-fledged, thriving city, with all the growing pains of other cities. It had changed. And the Athletic Club had changed with it. But it had not lost its link to the past.

Shortly before his death Bill Street said, "The old club was such a great club — the Adairs, the Leides, the Maxwells. People make up the club, of course. As long as we've carried the same people with us, it's still the same club. A lifetime of members is what we are really talking about."

For the clubs that history remembers, however, it is not a lifetime for a single generation. It's a lifetime for another generation, and another. Only the clubs that adapt to change yet retain enough values to keep their identity — the clubs that prove they are more than bricks and mortar — can serve members in that way. The Atlanta Athletic Club is one of those clubs.

L — R: Mrs. Walter Clifton, Past Presidents F.M. "Buster" Bird and Walter L. Clifton and Mrs. F.M. Bird.

In 1977 the Athletic Club celebrated its 75th anniversary. Past presidents and their wives were honored. L — R: Past

Presidents Mr. & Mrs. Ira H. Hardin, Mr. & Mrs. Walter L. Clifton and Mr. & Mrs. H. C. "Hikie" Allen.

117

COURSE LAYOUT

*Riverside and Highlands
Courses showing renovations
on Highlands to be completed
by July 1988.*

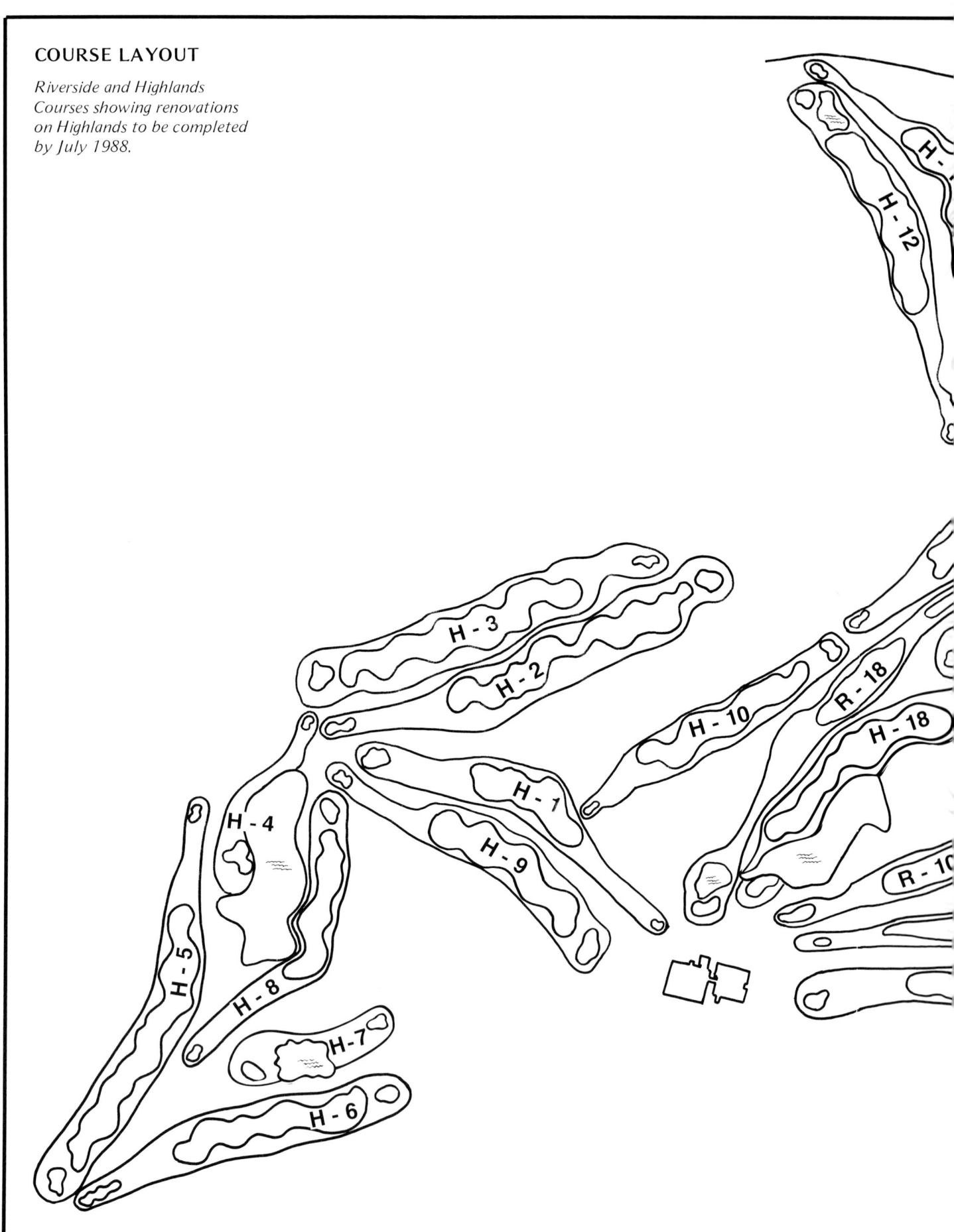

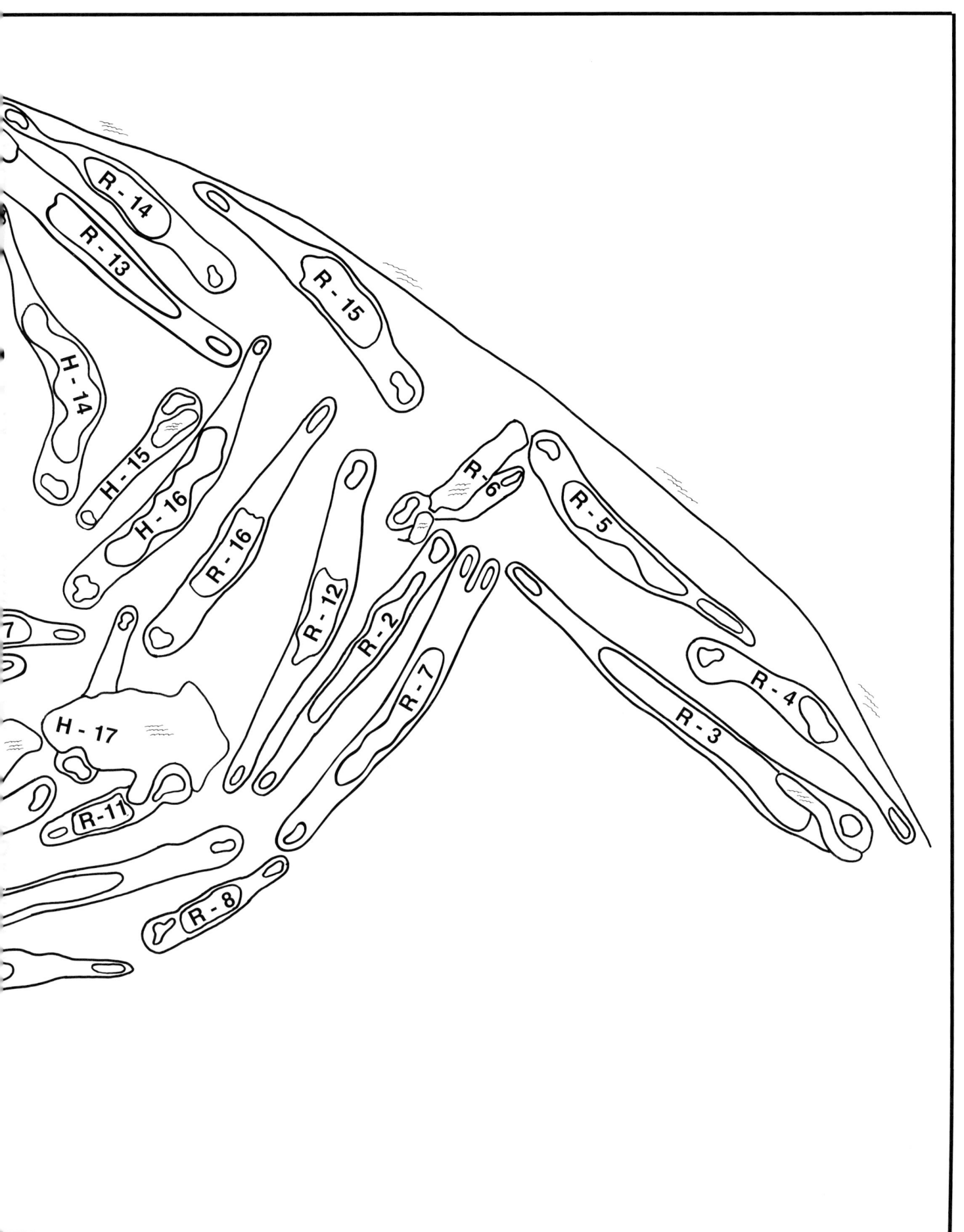

RIVERSIDE # 9
PAR 4

Champ. 453 yds. hdcp. 9
Mens   412 yds. hdcp. 9
Ladies 346 yds.

This is one of the most challenging holes on the Riverside course. It is a combination of both length and accuracy. Besides pine trees lining both sides of the fairway, an added peril is O.B. on the left. A fairway bunker is strategically located on the right side of the fairway with mounds lining the driving area on the left; therefore, it is extremely important to drive the ball straight. Not only is a good drive essential, but the second shot must be hit with a long iron or fairway wood into a two-tiered green guarded by two large bunkers on the front left and a bunker on the right.

HIGHLANDS #3
PAR 4

Champ. 470 yds. hdcp. 1
Mens   432 yds. hdcp. 1
Ladies 322 yds. hdcp. 7

Always one of the toughest holes on the course. The length of the hole is a contributing factor to its difficulty. A good tee shot is essential as the ball must be played down the left middle of the fairway in an attempt to keep the ball safely away from a ravine filled with trees on the left. The second shot requires a long iron or fairway wood to a green well guarded on all sides by bunkers.

HIGHLANDS #15
PAR 3

Champ. 218 yds. hdcp. 10
Mens   172 yds. hdcp. 10
Ladies 135 yds. hdcp. 16

This was the third most difficult hole during the 1976 U.S. Open and 1981 P.G.A. Championships. The tee is elevated and guarded by tall pines which line the fairway. The green is guarded by a pond on the right side and a bunker on the left. These factors, along with the length, combine to create the difficulty of this hole. An accurate tee shot is needed as most players will attempt to aim the ball toward the left side of the green in order to stay away from the water on the right.

CHRONOLOGY OF KEY EVENTS

1898   First organizational meeting
Granting of club charter

1899   Official opening of 56 Edgewood Avenue facility

1902   Move to new clubhouse at 37 Auburn Avenue

1904   Purchase of East Lake property

1908   Opening of East Lake Country Club and expanded golf course

1914   Destruction of East Lake clubhouse by fire

1915   Opening of new clubhouse and restructured course at East Lake

1924   Purchase of Carnegie Way property

1925   Destruction of East Lake clubhouse by fire

1926   Opening of Carnegie Way town club
Opening of new East Lake clubhouse

1928   Purchase of property for "Number Two" golf course

1930   Winning of Grand Slam by Bobby Jones

1950   Hosting of U.S. Women's Amateur
Addition of new wing (with dancing terrace) at East Lake

1957   Opening of Yacht Club site for use

1958   Formal opening of Lake Lanier Yacht Club
Addition of swimming pool at East Lake

1962   Hosting of Southern Badminton Championship

1963   Purchase of River Bend property

1966   Sale of "Number Two Course" at East Lake

1967   Opening of new 27-hole golf course at River Bend

1968   Vote by stockholders to sell East Lake Country Club

1969   Selection of Atlanta Athletic Club Country Club as name for River Bend club

1970   Opening of new country club facility at River Bend
Opening of Tennis facility at River Bend

1971   Decision to sell Carnegie Way town club
Closing of Carnegie Way town club

1973   Destruction of Carnegie Way town club
Addition of social wing to country club
Opening of new Athletic Center at River Bend

1976   Hosting of U.S. Open
Opening of Robert T. Jones, Jr., Memorial Room
First Annual Sports Appreciation Night

1979   First Annual 10-Kilometer Run
Hosting of Southern Badminton Tournament

1980   50th Anniversary of Grand Slam

1981   Hosting of PGA Championship

1982   Hosting of Junior World Cup Tournament
First Annual Basketball Clinic

1983   Opening of indoor tennis center
Opening of redesigned clubhouse
First Annual Pops Concert

1984   Hosting of USGA Mid-Amateur Championship
Hosting of National Senior Racquetball Tournament

1985   Hosting of U.S. Badminton Association Championship

1986   Dedication of Royal Troon Room to Charlie Yates
Selection of AAC as host for 1990 U.S. Women's Open

NOTABLE ACHIEVEMENTS BY AAC
GOLFERS

Perry Adair
    Southern Amateur, 1921, 1923
Thomas W. Barnes, Sr.
    Southern Four-ball Winner, 1940, 1941, 1946,
        1947
    Southern Amateur, 1947, 1949
Watts Gunn
    U.S. Amateur, runner-up, 1925
    U.S. Intercollegiate, 1927
    Southern Amateur, 1928
    Southern Open, 1928
Charles W. Harrison
    Southern Amateur, 1955
Helen D. Lowndes
    Southern Women's Amateur, 1922, 1924
Robert T. Jones, Jr.
    Southern Amateur, 1917, 1920, 1922
    U.S. Amateur, 1924, 1925, 1927, 1928, 1930
    U.S. Open, 1923, 1926, 1929, 1930
    British Amateur, 1930
    British Open, 1926, 1927, 1930
    GRAND SLAM, 1930
Dorothy Kirby (honorary member)
    U.S. Women's Amateur, 1951
Martha Wilkinson Kirouac
    U.S. Women's Amateur, 1972
Margaret Maddox
    Southern Women's Amateur, 1929
Larry Nelson (honorary member)
    PGA Championship, 1981
Jerry Pate (honorary member)
    U.S. Open, 1976
Michael Podolak (honorary member)
    U.S.G.A. Mid-Amateur Championship, 1984
Alexa Stirling
    Southern Women's Amateur, 1915, 1916,
        1920
    U.S. Women's Amateur, 1916, 1919, 1920
    Canadian Women's Amateur, 1920, 1924
Louise Suggs (honorary member)
    Southern Women's Amateur, 1941
    Western Women's Open, 1947
    Western Women's Amateur, 1947
    GRAND SLAM, 1948
    British Ladies Amateur, 1948
Charles R. Yates
    U.S. Intercollegiate Champion, 1934
    Western Amateur, 1935
    British Amateur, 1938

PRESIDENTS

(and year elected)

Burton Smith 1898
Arnold Broyles 1903
George W. Adair 1905
J. H. Porter 1912
Asa G. Candler, Jr. 1915
John W. Bachman 1917
Scott Hudson 1919
Robert P. Jones 1937
Henry C. Heinz 1942
E. A. Thornwell 1943
Robert T. Jones, Jr. 1946
T. R. Garlington 1947
W. B. Farnsworth 1949
A. D. Boylston, Jr. 1951
Watts Gunn 1953
Hugh M. Dorsey, Jr. .1955
Ira H. Hardin 1957
Walter L. Clifton, Jr. .1959
F. M. Bird 1961
H. C. Allen, Jr. 1963
Larry P. Martin 1965
Allen S. Hardin 1968
Eugene T. Branch 1970
L. Glenn Dewberry, Jr. 1972
W. W. Gaston 1974
George W. Brodnax, III 1976
Graydon Hall 1978
Merriell Autrey, Jr. 1980
John P. Imlay, Jr. 1982
Don W. Sands 1984
J. Neal Purcell 1986

YACHT CLUB COMMODORES

1957	Hal A. Cook	1972	Richard K. Whitehead
1958	Charles Haasl	1973	George H. Brodnax, III
1959	J. Ross Hanahan	1974	George H. Brodnax, III
1960	E. L. Chipman	1975	L. Glenn Dewberry, Jr.
1961	E. L. Chipman	1976	Paul M. Flood
1962	Asa W. Candler	1977	Paul M. Flood
1963	Asa W. Candler	1978	Paul M. Flood
1964	Larry P. Martin	1979	Charles W. McDowell, Jr.
1965	Larry P. Martin	1980	William A. Canning
1966	M. Oliver Saggus	1981	William A. Canning
1967	M. Oliver Saggus	1982	William A. Canning
1968	M. Oliver Saggus	1983	Jack R. Kelly, Jr.
1969	M. Oliver Saggus	1984	Jack R. Kelly, Jr.
1970	M. Oliver Saggus	1985	Lawrence H. Garrett
1971	L. Glenn Dewberry, Jr.	1986	Ron R. Harding

1987-88 COMMITTEES

Administration/Personnel
W. Glenn Cornell
J. Neal Purcell
Gaylord O. Coan
William J. Goldin
John L. Johnson
Thomas J. Martin
Michael C. Murphy

Athletics
Paul R. Dean
Ron R. Harding
Robert J. Bartkow
James R. Braden
Michael W. Broadbear
George H. Brodnax IV
J. W. Holderfield
Mrs. Larry (Carol) O'Connor
B. J. Strong
R. L. Tindol III
W. P. West
Thomas M. Wilson

Construction
Ron R. Harding
Don W. Sands
Marvin M. Black
Bill Karl Bryant
W. Michael Caldwell
William H. Childress
Carlton P. Fountain
James G. Richardson
John H. Wiedeman

Finance
Rene V. Cote
W. Glenn Cornell
Gaylord O. Coan
F. E. Meason
James C. McMeen
John I. Mitchell
Harold B. Todd, Jr.
Larry L. Turner
Wayne W. Woody

Golf Pro Shop
Jack R. Kelly, Jr.
Paul R. Dean
Gary O. Alberson
David W. Dorman
Thomas F. Forkner
Wade H. Mayo
Larry O'Connor, Jr.

Charles C. Pittard, Jr.
Larry L. Turner
Wayne W. Woody

Golf Grounds
Edmund W. Jones
Harvey R. Holding
O. P. Ackerman, Jr.
D. Cary Allen
H. Norman Atkins
Frank M. Deaver
Robert R. Kirouac
William F. Nygaard
William G. Pierce
James P. Trimble
Richard H. Waters

Golf Pro Shop
Jack R. Kelly, Jr.
Paul R. Dean
Gary O. Alberson
David W. Dorman
Thomas F. Forkner
Wade H. Mayo
Larry O'Connor, Jr.
Charles C. Pittard, Jr.
William R. Short
James F. Teate
Mrs. J. C. (Joanne) Wampler
John W. Wells

Govt. Public Affairs/Zoning
William L. O'Callaghan, Jr.
Don W. Sands
Thomas B. Fowler, Jr.
Donald F. Mairose
Charles E. Reiley
T. Cole Van Houten

House
Larry H. Garrett
Edmund W. Jones
Dean E. Beauregard
Don E. Burleson
Jerry Chapman
F. T. Christian
Geoffrey R. Crabbe
E. E. Dyson
E. Craig French
J. Thomas Humphries
Howard O. Moore, Jr.
George W. Sands

Long Range Planning
Jack R. Kelly, Jr.
J. Neal Purcell
Merriell Autrey, Jr.
Eugene T. Branch
George H. Brodnax III
Charles R. Brown
L. Glenn Dewberry, Jr.
Charles L. Douglas, Jr.
John P. Imlay, Jr.
L. Harold Williams

Membership/Communications
William L. Callaghan, Jr.
Larry H. Garrett
Gordon R. Bailey
W. Chapman Crawford
Howard L. Crispin
Louis J. Douglas III
James R. Harrison
J. Robert Lester
James E. Pudvin
John M. Stanley
Hal W. Watts

Tennis
Harvey R. Holding
William L. O'Callaghan, Jr.
Thomas M. Backman
Mrs. Wm. A. (Bev) Cheek, Jr.
Steve J. Davis
Mrs. Paul M. (June) Flood
Donald E. Hall
William G. Miller
John K. Totten
Lowell W. White, Jr.
Mrs. L. W. (Toni) White, Jr.
Frank F. Wicker

Yacht Club
Ron R. Harding
Rene V. Cote
J. Chandler Baldwin, Jr.
John H. Christian
Gordon O. Cope
Paul A. Ebbs, Jr.
Peter H. Giles
J. Randall Garner
Paul C. Hanna
Patrick M. Thomas
Walter T. Sale
John L. Underwood III

CLUB CHAMPIONS

Singles Club Badminton Champions
1980	Robert L. Johnson
1981	William R. Lassiter, Jr.
1982	William R. Lassiter, Jr.
1983	Robert L. Johnson
1984	Robert L. Johnson
1985	Robert L. Johnson
1986	Robert L. Johnson

Club Golfing Champions
1907	F. G. Byrd
1908	F. G. Byrd
1909	W. R. Tichenor
1910	W. R. Tichenor
1911	H. G. Scott
1912	G. H. Atkisson
1913	George W. Adair
1914	Perry Adair
1915	Robert T. Jones, Jr.
1916	Robert T. Jones, Jr.
1917	Robert T. Jones, Jr.
1921	Richard L. Hickey
1923	Gene Cook
1924	Chick Ridley
1925	Watts Gunn
1928	Scott Hudson, Jr.
1929	Scott Hudson, Jr.
1930	Charles R. Yates
1931	Berrien Moore, Jr.
1932	Scott Hudson, Jr.
1933	Scott Hudson, Jr.
1934	T. R. Garlington
1935	Cliff McCaughey
1936	Morton Campbell, Jr.
1937	Thomas W. Barnes, Sr.
1938	Dan Yates
1939	Thomas W. Barnes, Sr.
1940	Ralph McCelland, Jr.
1941	Dr. Wm. C. Warren, Jr.
1942	C. H. McGaughey
1945	Rev. Pierce Harris
1946	Luke M. Barnes
1947	Luke M. Barnes
1948	Luke M. Barnes
1949	Alan Yates
1950	Watts Gunn
1951	Charles W. Harrison
1952	Alan Yates
1953	Watts Gunn
1954	Charles W. Harrison
1955	L. B. Roane, Jr.
1956	Pierce Miller
1957	Charles W. Harrison
1958	Robert Pierce
1959	Charles W. Harrison
1960	Charles W. Harrison
1961	Charles W. Harrison
1962	Charles W. Harrison
1963	Thomas W. Barnes, Jr.
1964	Thomas W. Barnes, Jr.
1965	Charles W. Harrison
1966	Thomas W. Barnes, Jr.
1967	Asby Taylor
1968	Charles W. Harrison
1969	Richard H. Waters
1970	Richard H. Waters
1971	William H. Beavers
1972	Richard H. Waters
1973	Edmund W. Jones, D.D.S.
1974	Charles R. Hastie
1975	Robert B. Sams
1976	Patrick M. Ford
1977	patrick M. Ford
1978	Patrick M. Ford
1979	Albert K. Everett, Jr.
1980	Gregory E. Stuhler
1981	Gregory E. Stuhler
1982	Gregory E. Stuhler
1983	Gregory E. Stuhler
1984	G. Steven McKnight
1985	Richard H. Waters
1986	Robert B. Sams

Club Women's Golfing Champions
1970	Eleanor Walker
1971	Eleanor Walker
1972	Eleanor Walker
1973	Cile Godwin
1974	Eleanor Walker
1975	Kay Smith
1976	Eleanor Walker
1977	Eleanor Walker
1978	Eleanor Walker
1979	Eleanor Walker
1980	Eleanor Walker
1981	Eleanor Walker
1982	Eleanor Walker
1983	Bette Sims
1985	Martha Kirouac
1986	Martha Kirouac

Club Handball Champions
1980	no tournament held
1981	Joe N. Guy
1982	Harry P. Siebold, Jr.
1983	William L. Hale
1984	Joe N. Guy
1985	no tournament held
1986	no tournament held

Club Racquetball Champions
1980	Jerry G. Wickliffe
1981	Jerry G. Wickliffe
1982	Jerry G. Wickliffe
1983	Jerry G. Wickliffe
1984	Michael P. Ganote
1985	Michael P. Ganote
1986	Charles P. Garrison, M.D.

Club Squash Champions
1980	William R. Lassiter, Jr.
1981	William R. Lassiter, Jr.
1982	W. Jeffrey Torrence
1983	W. Jeffrey Torrence
1984	Jerry G. Wickliffe
1985	W. Jeffrey Torrence
1986	W. Jeffrey Torrence

Club Singles Tennis Champions
1971*	L. Hill Griffin, M.D.
1972	Walter Johnson
1973	Rod Carlyle
1974	Rod Carlyle
1975	Keith Richardson
1976	W. R. Hardcastle, M.D.
1977	W. R. Hardcastle, M.D.
1978	W. R. Hardcastle, M.D.
1979	L. Hill Griffin, M.D.
1980	Steve J. Davis
1981	L. Hill Griffin, M.D.
1982	Steve J. Davis
1983	L. Hill Griffin, M.D.
1984	Jerry F. Ramano
1985	Jack Anderson
1986	Louis A. Barber

*The club's first annual invitational held at the northside country club in 1971.

CHARTER MEMBERS

George W. Adair, Jr.
Clifford L. Anderson
John D. Berry
Arnold Broyles
Milton Dargan
J. F. Dickinson
Preston Gilbert
Jack J. Hastings
A. M. Hoke
Joel Hurt
H. S. Jackson
W. R. Joyner
A. C. Keely
J. E. Lappert
Sanders McDaniel
V. A. Moore
A. J. Orme
W. L. Peel
Charles I. Ryan
R. F. Shedden
J. B. Stewart
Henry Thornton

H. M. Atkinson
Lowry Arnold
H. L. DeGive
Richard E. Bell
R. O. Campbell
James W. English, Jr.
C. H. Godfrey
R. G. Hartsfield
Frank Holland
George F. Hurt
M. M. Jackson
Logan Jones
Clarence Knowles
R. F. Maddox, Jr.
J. R. McKeldin
A. C. Morris
J. S. Owens
J. H. Porter
W. B. Roberts
Harry Silverman
H. O. Teat
Frank Wynne

U. S. Atkinson
S. Barnett
Clyde Brooks
Sol N. Clarke
George J. Dexter
Thomas B. Felder, Jr.
R. C. Hayden
William P. Hill
Albert Howell, Jr.
W. H. Inman
Harvey Johnson
Gordon P. Kiser
W. M. Leary
W. A. Matthews
Daniel McGill
James F. O'Neil
J. Carroll Payne
L. D. T. Quinby
H. L. Stearns
Burton Smith
Harry N. Taylor

STOCKHOLDING MEMBERS

Andrew J. Abernathy
George T. Achille
Joe T. Acker
Oliver P. Ackerman, Jr.
Forrest L. Adair II
Floyd P. Adams, Jr.
J. Davis Adams, Jr.
Thomas C. Adderhold
Thomas R. Agnew
King V. Aiken
L. J. Akin
Gary O. Alberson
Jerome B. Alexander
Billy C. Alford
Kenneth D. Alger
James W. Allbritten
D. Cary Allen
G. Millard Allen Jr.
Hiram C. Allen III
Julian D. Allen
Kenneth M. Allen
Wm. R. Allmond
Dr. H. W. Allsup
Jose E. Almeida
Stephen Earle Almond
William J. Alvarez
Charles O. Anderson
Douglas Anderson
Jack Anderson
James C. H. Anderson
James P. Anderson
James W. Anderson, Jr.
John B. Anderson
Edward B. Andrews
Richard F. Andrews
L. Richard Anheuser
W.S. (Bill) Ansley, Jr.
Hisham A. Araim
A. Douglas Armstrong
Charles W. Armstrong
Robert S. Armstrong
Donald Harry Artinger
Rufus C. Ashworth
H. Norman Atkins
T. Mayo Atkins DDS
Lt. Tim H. Atkins
Rudolf W. August
Glenn T. Austin
Thomas F. Austin, Jr.
W. Herrin Austin
Walter T. Austin
Merriell Autrey, Jr.
C. G. Aycock, Jr.
John C. Ayers
M. Dee Babcock
Wesley G. Bacastow
D. Ernest Bacon, Jr.
John R. Baer
O. J. Baggarly
James M. Bahin
Gordon R. Bailey
James G. Bailey
Paul L. Bailey
William H. Baine
Jonathan C. Baker
Terry J. Baker
Angelo C. Baldi
J. Chandler Baldwin, Jr.
James B. Ballard
Larry A. Ballew
Louis Angelo Barber
J. F. Barlow, D.D.S.
Alan L. Barnes
Arthur W. Barnes
Thomas W. Barnes, Jr.
Richard G. Barnett
E. Stanley Barnwell
E. C. Barrett
Sidney R. Barrett
Chip Barron, Jr.
George W. Barron, Sr.

Jesse E. Barrow
Thomas M. Barry
Robert J. Bartkow
Wm. F. Baughn
Erwin G. Baumer
John Douglas Bays
Richard G. Beard
David L. Beason, D.O.
Dean E. Beauregard
Thomas M. Beckman
James M. Beeson, Jr.
George V. Belkofer, Jr.
Frank P. Bell
John L. Bell, Jr.
Theodore Benning, Jr.
S. Jack Benson
Thomas S. Bentley
Reuben M. Berry, Jr.
Samuel M. Berry, III
Robert L. Berto
Robert L. Bilton
Richard Binion III
Michael H. Biondo
Francis M. Bird
Lloyd D. Bird
Robert R. Bischoff
Arthur M. Bishop
Robert D. Bishop
Robert A. Bittner
Marvin M. Black
Michael M. Black
Ralph E. Black
Thomas J. Black
W. R. Black
John T. Blackburn
M. H. Blackshear
Henry H. Blake
C. W. Blalock, Jr.
Thomas C. Blaska
Boyd J. Blevins
William P. Blincoe
Brice Bloodgood
Col. Earl Bodron
George E. Boehm
B. Frank Boggs
Samuel K. Bohler
Kenneth C. Bollinger
Philip T. Bolt
Howard M. Bone
John K. Bonnell
Frank M. Boorn
William H. Booth III
James L. Borck
William K. Borland
Donald L. Bosshardt
W. L. Bost
Robert S. Bostic
Joe D. Bourn
J. M. Bowden
David R. Bowen
Kenneth H. Bowman, Jr.
Albert L. Boyd, Jr.
Raymond A. Boyer
John G. Boyette
A. D. Boylston, Jr.
Robert W. Boylston, Sr.
A. Thomas Bradbury
James R. Braden
Dr. Thomas Bragg
Eugene T. Branch
Eugene T. Branch, Jr.
John E. Branch
R. L. Brand, Jr.
Warner E. Brand
John R. Brannen
George E. Brannon
W. C. Braswell
Guy C. Brazell, Jr.
Joseph B. Brennan
Alvin L. Bridges, Jr.
George D. Bridges

Tommy H. Bridges
James Amos Brigman, Jr. MD
Royce Britt
Michael W. Broadbear
Edward P. Broadbear
John A. Brocksmith
George H. Brodnax III
Marcus E. Bromley
Eugene D. Brooks
Eugene E. Brooks
Gordon E. Brooks, Sr.
James Donald Brooks
James W. Brooks, Jr.
George C. Broome, Jr.
Gary W. Bross
Adrian W. Brown
Charles R. Brown
David M. Brown
Edward J. Brown
Harvey G. Brown
James W. Brown
John R. Brown
John W. Brown
Lester A. Brown, M.D.
Rudy A. Brown
Theron R. Brown
Walter S. Brown
Marvin J. Brownlee
John Alfred Broyles, III, M.D.
Milton J. Bruce
Mark H. Bruder
Horace Brumit
Don Bryan, Jr.
William D. Bryan, Sr.
Bill Karl Bryant
Lawrence J. Buchwald
A. M. Buckler, Jr.
J. S. Buckler, D.M.D.
Stanley J. Budzik
Roy V. Bullard
Stan R. Bullington
Robert F. Bullock
B. B. Bundesman, Jr.
Donald E. Burleson
Keith N. Burleson
Roy B. Burnette
Harris S. Burns, Jr.
Richard J. Burrell
H. E. Burroughs
William S. Burt
David L. Burton
Donald G. Burton
Jack Burton
Edward B. Burwell
Robert C. Bush
Sydney H. Bush
W. D. Caldwell
W. Michael Caldwell
T. M. Callaway
James W. Callison
Jack J. Camarda
Thomas L. Camp
Charles W. Campbell
G. M. Campbell
Randall W. Campbell
Thomas H. Campbell III
Scott Candler, Jr.
William A. Canning
Thomas A. Cantrell, Jr.
George W. Carah
Owen F. Cardell, Jr.
Judge George H. Carley
Michael C. Carlos
Hubert M. Carmichael
Robert D. Carney
J. Robert Carpenter
Richard W. Carpenter
Robert E. Carpenter
James C. Carr, Sr.
Julian S. Carr
J. Randall Carroll

John W. Carroll, Jr.
John D. Carson, M.D.
Don E. Carter
Patrick T. Casey
William Peter Casey
Harry L. Cashin, Jr.
Stuart A. Cashin, Jr.
David H. Cavan
Joseph A. Cerniglia
Joseph T. Cerniglia
Vitya Chakrabandhu
Jack L. Chambers
R. M. Chambers
R. Carl Chandler
Jerry Chapman
Paul H. Chapman
Thomas F. Chapman
T. Z. Chastain
Clayton D. Chatham
R. Pierce Chatham
R. T. Chatham
Raymond T. Chatham, Jr.
William A. Cheek, II
Joseph Cheeley, Jr.
B. H. Cherry
John D. Chesnut
C. L. Childers
William H. Childress
Garland L. Childrey
Dennis M. Chorba
F. T. "Tim" Christian
John H. Christian
Wm. David Christian
Neil Christman
Alan D. Chunka
Walter B. Church
John S. Churchill
Charles D. Clark
Paul A. Clark
William L. Clarke
Kenneth B. Clary
J. V. Clement
Louie W. Cleveland
Robert G. Clevenger
Thomas G. Cloud
Melvin B. Coalson
Gaylord O. Coan
Paul Cobb, Jr.
Cliff M. Cochran
James D. Cofer, Jr.
E. J. Cogburn, Jr.
J. Olin Coile
J. Grady Coleman
Oscar H. Coleman
Douglas A. Collins
William R. Collins, Jr.
Peter C. Collura
James E. Combee
George R. Coney, Jr.
Robert S. Conley
Leo H. Connors
Edward C. Conrad
James C. Conrads
David C. Cook, Jr.
Jim R. Cook
Charles L. Cooley, DDS
James H. Cooley, Jr.
O. Gordon Cope
James E. Copeland, Jr.
Robert C. Copeland
Steve E. Copeland
Robert A. Corbitt
John J. Corley, Jr.
W. Glenn Cornell
Maury H. Corp
Guy F. Costabile
Alton M. Costley
Rene V. Cote
S. A. Council
James C. Cowart
John H. Cowart

128

Benjamin G. Cox
John F. Coyne III
Geoffrey R. Crabbe
James F. Craig, Jr.
Guy Curtis Crain
C. L. Crawford, M.D.
Harry N. Crawford, Jr.
Thomas J. Crawford
W. Chapman Crawford
James A. Creech, Jr.
Herbert L. Creecy
Val G. Crelia
E. Ray Crim, Jr.
Robert C. Crim
Howard L. Crispin
John W. Criss
Donald J. Crossley
B. W. Crosswell
L. Terry Crouch
James E. Crouse
Carroll L. Crowther
Tom U. Crumpton III
Richard H. Culberson
David A. Cunningham, Jr.
Peter J. Curnin
John E. Curry
Ronald W. Curry
John P. Curtis
Gordon W. Curtiss, Jr.
Terry L. Cusick
Benjamin M. Cutler
Duncan B. Cutler
Alan W. Dailey
Arthur Dana
Edwin C. Daniel
Richard C. Daniel
Charles E. Daniels
William D. Danielson
John R. Darnall
Donald B. Daves
Charles L. Davidson, Jr.
Charles L. Davidson, III
Carlyle T. Davis
Clifford A. Davis
E. B. Davis
J. C. Davis, M.D.
John C. Davis
Lafayette Davis
Philip P. Davis, Jr.
Robert E. Davis
Stanley R. Davis
Steve J. Davis
Donald W. Dawson
James M. Dawson
C. L. Deal
A. L. (Al) Dean, Jr.
G. Hilton Dean
Paul R. Dean
Frank M. Deaver
James M. Deavours
Loomis E. Deavours
Curtis I. Delany, Jr.
E. J. DeLay
Leonard R. DeLoach, Jr.
Frank S. DeLuca
Edward M. Dennett
Harold T. Denson
L. G. Dewberry, Jr.
Jack D. Deweese
William N. Dick
Robert L. Dickson
Talmadge F. Dickson
Joe D. Digby
J. Austin Dilbeck
Donald H. Dimmick
Louie C. Dodd
Curtis, J. Dolan
Robert F. Donegan
James W. Donnelly
Dennis J. Dorner
Donald J. Dorner
Hugh M. Dorsey, Jr.
R. Fred Doty
Chris H. Doughtie
Charles L. Douglas, Jr.
John L. Douglas
Louis J. Douglass III

Paul E. Drack
C. E. Drummond, Jr.
Charles S. Drummond
James W. DuBose, Jr.
Larry D. Duckett
Paul J. Duffy
Robert Y. Duke
Jack F. Dulaney
William W. Dunn
Gerald C. Durand
Ronald Durning
C. E. Dycus
Charles M. Dykes
F. E. Dyson
Robert W. Eaves, Jr.
Paul Allen Ebbs, Jr.
James R. Echols
H. Raymond Eckman
John P. Economou
Thomas K. Eddins, Jr.
G. F. Edwards, Sr.
William S. Edwards
Mack P. Efland, Jr.
William B. Eidson
James W. Ellis, Jr.
R. C. Ellison
Thomas L. Elsberry
Michael L. Ely
Alton J. Embry
James H. Embry
O'Neal Embry
Charles B. Emerson
John D. Engel, DDS
Stone T. Ermentrout
Richard G. Ernest
Joe A. Escott
Kent E. Evans
William R. Evans
A. L. Evatt, Jr., DDS
Richard E. Falkowski
James B. Fallaize
Michael E. Fallaize
John C. Falter
C. G. Farabee
M. T. (Tommy) Farmer
John B. Farra, Jr.
Milton C. Farris
Donald G. Fehrman
George R. Fellows
C. Scott Ferguson
Charles R. Ferguson
Paul R. Ferm
N. Lamar Ferrell
Elwyn E. Fike
E. Lanier Finch
Robert L. Fincher
Guy B. Findley
Edward A. Fingarson
Joseph C. Finley, MD
Jeff M. Fisher
Michael A. Fisher
Charles A. Fitzgerald
R. William Fitzgerald
Charlie B. Fiveash
Thomas T. Flagler
C. L. Flake, Jr.
Stephen J. Flanagan
Robert H. Fleming
G. Ross Flint
Paul M. Flood
Murray Lee Florence, Jr.
Richard A. Foote
Harold E. Ford
Harold F. Ford, Jr.
James Leroy Ford
Patrick M. Ford
William B. Ford
Thurber M. Foreman II
Thomas F. Forkner
Roy W. Forrester
Allan H. Forsyth
John W. Fortune
Andrew N. Foster, Jr.
Robert E. Foster, Jr.
W. Rufus Foster
Carlton P. Fountain
Albert C. Fowler, Jr.

Thomas B. Fowler, Jr.
W. V. Fox
Benjamin C. Frankland
Fred D. Franklin
Richard P. Fraser
Guy W. Freeman
William A. Freeman
A. H. Fregosi, M.D.
John G. Freihaut
Edgar Craig French
Louis M. Frick
John Scott Frost
Stephen A. Furbacher
Thomas W. Gable, M.D.
Ralph Gabrielson
G. K. Gaddis
William H. Gaik
John G. Gammage
Dock E. Gammage
R. Gentry Ganote
Robert D. Garces
J. Earl Gardner
Jerry G. Gardner
J. Randell Garner
C. Kirk Garrett
Lawrence H. Garrett
William B. Garrett
Charles P. Garrison, M.D.
Thomas C. Garrity
Paul K. Garver
Finely Garvin, D.D.S.
William W. Gaston
W. Wylie Gaston IV
John H. Gemmill
George H. George
Ronald D. George
Lawrence T. Gibbs
Arthur H. Gifford, Jr.
John E. Gilbert
John Lockhart Gile
Peter H. Giles
Geoffrey C. Gill
Charles B. Ginden
Ronald A. Glah
Charles W. Glass
J. Wendell Glass, DDS
Thomas W. Gleason
Wilbur F. Glenn
John D. Glover
H. Fred Gober
William J. Goldin
David Goodchild, DDS
Edwin F. Goodman
Leonard Gordon, Jr.
Herbert I. Gordy
W. J. (Benny) Gouge, Jr.
Fred S. Gould
Richard C. Govan, Jr.
Bernard C. Governale
John C. Grable
Carl S. Graham
Charles E. Graham
John C. Graham, Jr.
B. Howard Grant, D.D.S.
Charles B. Grant
Charles M. Gray
Stanley E. Green
W. E. Green, Jr. M.D.
James L. Greene
Richard W. Greene
Ansel D. Greenway
Wm. Gary Gregg
Francis S. Gregory
Jack S. Griffin
L. H. Griffin, M.D.
Marion Lee Griffin
A. W. Griffith
John L. Griffith
Lee B. Griffith
James C. Grizzard
Eugene R. Grotnes
Watts Gunn
Guy T. Gunter
Raymond C. Gunti
Don E. Gustavel
H. D. Guthrie
Samuel D. Guy

Mitchell Gwinn
Harold C. Haase, Jr.
John B. Hadley, Jr.
James G. Hagen
Charles D. Hailey
Claude J. Haines
Glenville Haldi
Robert W. Haldi
Jack W. Hale
James A. Hale
Rodney L. Hale
William L. Hale
Donald E. Hall
Graydon Hall
Grover T. Hall III Dr.
Hulan L. Hall
J. Harvey Hall
Jack M. Hall, Jr.
Robert C. Hall
Roger W. Hall
Thomas A. Hall
John F. Hallman, Jr.
Melvin C. Halstead
Daniel C. Halvorson
Donald P. Hamelink
James Roy Hamilton
William J. Hamilton, Jr.
William J. Hamilton III
J. Ross Hanahan
Warren E. Hanchey
W. R. Hancock
Walter E. Haney
M. Corbet Hankey
Richard O. Hanley
Paul C. Hanna, D.D.S.
Rolfe Millar Hanna
Magnus M. Hanson
Nolan T. Hanson
James Burett Haralson
Earl Olin Harbour
W. R. Hardcastle, M.D.
W. Leon Hardeman
Gary C. Harden
Allen S. Hardin
Ira H. Hardin
Ron R. Harding
Alfred M. Harp
J. P. Harrington, Jr.
James F. Harrington
Jack H. Harris
Charles W. Harrison
Ernest Harrison
Jack E. Harrison
James Richard Harrison
Morris E. Harrison, Jr.
Morris E. Harrison, Sr.
Robert F. Harrison
Daniel L. Hart
Don C. Hart
Donald C. Hart
Charles R. Hastie
Douglas P. Hatcher
Robert Hatfield
Edward J. Hauer
George Hauer
Dennis Carl Hayes
Hugh G. Head, Jr.
Ralph S. Healey
John P. Heard, M.D.
Robert R. Hearn
Raymond D. Hedberg
Robert Hedrick
Charles B. Hefner
William L. Heinz, Jr.
Philip Louis Helms
Roy K. Hendee
Bill Henderlight
Don G. Henderson
Robert J. Henderson
Russell G. Henderson
Ronald David Hendrix
M. E. Henley
Robert Ernest Hennig
Robert L. Henning
Elmon H. Henry
W. Barry Henry
William C. Henry

Thomas M. Hensley, Jr.
Hal M. Herd, M.D.
Dorsey Hester
Edward S. Heys
N. W. Heyward, Jr.
Ned W. Heyward
W. H. Heyward
Heyward, William L.
David J. Hickey
Curtis O. Hicks
Glenn E. Hicks, Jr.
William T. Hicks
Gale B. Highland
C. C. Hightower
Robert E. Hilburn
Eugene Hill, M.D.
Charles L. Hill
L. J. (Jay) Hill, Jr.
Roy S. Hill
A. Kenneth Hilley
Michael J. Hillmeyer
William J. Hirsch
Robert F. Hochman, Ph.D.
Robert J. Hodge
William S. Hodges
J. C. Hoffman, Jr., M.D.
William J. Hoffman
O. W. Hogan, Jr.
G. Scott Hogg
Jack B. Hogg
R. H. Hogg
Robert J. Holbrook
George Holcomb
Douglas A. Holder
James W. Holderfield
Harvey R. Holding
Robert L. Holley
J. R. Hollingsworth
Otis Jack Holloman
Chester Clay Holloway, III
Gene T. Holloway
John R. Holman
Robert F. Holman
Robert F. Holman, Jr.
W. E. Honey, Jr.
Boyd B. Hood
George W. Hood
A. R. Hooks, Jr.
George B. Hooks
Duane L. Hoover
Charles E. Hopper
William E. Hopper, Jr.
Henry T. Hornsby
Howard M. Horton
Len Hoshall
Larry Val Houston
Robert B. Houston
Evan H. Housworth
W. Kent Hovis, D.C.
C. K. Howard, M.D.
Clarence I. Howard
David C. Howard
George M. Howard
Henry G. Howard, Jr.
James C. Howard, Jr.
John A. Howard, Jr.
Hugh H. Howell, Jr.
George F. Hubbert
Samuel L. Hubbs
D. Scott Hudgens
Mark R. Hudgens
Michael S. Hudgens
Louis D. Hudson, Jr.
Robert H. Hudson
Claude L. Huey, Jr.
Travis G. Huffines
William S. Huggins
Bradford N. Hughes
Howard R. Hughes, Jr.
Robert W. Hughes
Colias J. Hulsey
Jerry B. Hulsey
Herbert M. Humphrey
J. Thomas Humphries
Wm. B. Hundley, Jr.
E. R. Hunter
William T. Huntley

Willard P. Hurst, Jr.
Charles F. Hurston
Dallas A. Hurston
Kenneth M. Husler
Charles H. Hyatt
Carl O. Hyde, Jr.
John T. Hydrick, M.D.
John P. Imlay, Jr.
John F. Ingram, Jr.
Clarence B. Irwin, Jr.
Charles E. Jabaley
Fred A. Jabaley, D.D.S.
Charles A. Jackson, Jr.
Daniel H. Jackson
Frank D. Jackson
George E. Jackson
Harold F. Jackson
James E. Jackson
Rodney F. Jackson
William W. Jackson
Richard E. Jakubecy
T. Allen James, D.D.S.
Joe R. Jamison
James J. Jardina
Raymond H. Jarvis
Patrick R. Jenkins
C. B. Jennings, Jr.
Peter A. Jensen, Jr. D.D.S.
Jack F. Jericho
Ralph W. Jernigan, Jr.
Phillip H. Jessup
William J. Jewell
Jerry L. Jiles
Thomas L. Johns, Jr.
Charles G. Johnson
Donald A. Johnson
Earl W. Johnson, Jr.
Floyd A. Johnson
G. Fred Johnson
John L. Johnson
N. R. Johnson
Richard M. Johnson
Robert L. Johnson
W. A. Johnson, Jr.
Wm. L. Johnson, Jr.
Jack M. Johnston
Nesbit Johnston
Robert L. Johnston
Richard J. Jokl
Charles H. Jones
Cleve R. Jones, D.D.S.
D. Christie Jones
David R. Jones
Edmund W. Jones, D.D.S.
Glower W. Jones
J. W. Jones
Ralph J. Jones
Robert P. Jones, Jr.
Samuel L. Jones
Stephen M. Jones
Stuart M. Jones
Walter A. Jones
Charles R. Jordan
Fred L. Jordan
W. D. Jordan, M.D.
Jordan P. Jung
E. W. Justice, M.D.
Lee E. Karschner
Lloyd Lee Karschner
W. Gordon Kay
M. R. Kays, Jr.
Richard C. Kellogg
Jack R. Kelly, Jr.
James P. Kelly, Jr.
James R. Kelly, III
Jerry T. Kendall
Edward J. Kennedy
Lamar Kennedy
Lee Kennedy
Louis L. Kennedy
Jack N. Kenney
Donald E. Kern
Richard C. Kerns
Samuel W. Kiker
Nobles L. Killebrew
Cliff C. Kimsey, III
Earl W. King

Harry L. King, Jr.
John Hill King
Louis E. King
Michael G. King
J. W. Kingery
Ronald P. Kirby
Robert R. Kirouac
Gordon P. Kiser, Jr.
Joel J. Knight, Jr.
Clyde B. Knipfer
Eugene B. Knippers
Louis H. Koch
Conrad D. Kohlman
John Bradford Koontz
William G.Kooymans
Kenneth Korff
Thomas A. Kowalewski
Douglas F. Kraft
William J. Kramer
Carl L. Kranig
Ronald J. Krause
Alan M. Kuehn, D.D.S.
Frank E. Kutcher, Jr.
John Curtis Kyle, Jr.
Joe T. LaBoon
T. B. Lance
Henry E. Lane
Marshall R. Lane
Richard Asher
Ronald H. Lane
I. Ward Lang
Wm. R. Lassiter, Jr.
James B. Lathom
John M. Law
E. Jack Lawrence
Van C. Leach
D. Dale Leake
Jack W. Leathers
J. H. Ledbetter
W. J. Lee
William C. Lee
John Lemasters III
J. Robert Lester
John H. Levergood
Charles D. Lewis, Jr.
Willis E. Lewis
D. A. Liegerot, Sr.
Gary Light
Aubrey H. Liles, Jr.
Peyton I. Lingle
Walter C. Liss, Jr.
Guy E. Lites, Jr.
Guy E. Lites III
Tommie L. Little
H. Dave Livsey
Jack H. Logan
Dean L. Long
Harold Boyd Long, Jr.
Thomas R. Long
Thomas R. Long, Ph.D.
William T. Long
C. Linden Longino, Jr.
J. L. Longino
James M. Luckey, Jr.
Donald R. Luger
Jerry S. Lund
Robert T. Lusk
Carl G. Lusted
Homer J. Lynskey
Harold L. Machen
Dan Macrenaris
E. G. Macrenaris
Paul C. Maddox
Donald G. Maffett
Charles M. Magbee
Charles M. Magbee, Jr.
James M. Magee
Donald F. Mairose
John W. Maki
Woodie B. Malone, Jr.
Irvin W. Maloney
William A. Mamrack
Andrew J. Mangione
William L. Markert III
M. J. Markey, M.D.
William E. Marriott
William Marshall, D.D.S.

H. Fielder Martin
Jack Martin
Jack R. Martin
Jon S. Martin
Michael W. Martin
Thomas J. Martin
Wm. Homer Martin
Claude D. Mason
J. Alex Mason
James D. Mason
Miles H. Mason, Jr., MD
Miles H. Mason, III, MD
Joseph C. Massee, M.D.
Julian L. Massey
Patrick L. Mathis
Harold Carl Mauney, Jr.
Weyman H. Maxey, Sr.
Alva G. Maxwell
James H. Maxwell
Donald G. Mayhall
Jerry Mack Maynard
Wade H. Mayo
John C. Mayson
Robert E. McAfee
W. J. McAlpin
John E. McCabe, Jr.
John E. McCabe II
Robert A. McCall
Robert E. McCallum
Jerry L. McCarn
J. Michael McCarthy
David M. McCarty
Edward M. McCarvey
H. B. McCauley, Jr.
Lee Royce McClary
J. Ralph McClelland
David N. McClung
Lee R. McClure
Dale L. McCord, M.D.
James A. McCormick
Joe M. McCormick
Jerry N. McCoy
William C. McCoy
Robert J. McCreary, Sr.
Charles McCrory, D.D.S.
C. F. McCuiston, M.D.
Wilton C. McCullers
Francis M. McCullough
Douglas N. McCurdy, Jr.
Walter P. McCurdy, Jr.
G. Pierce McCurry
Joseph A. McDade
Matthew F. McDaniel
Morris I. McDonald
Charles McDowell, Jr., M.D.
A. P. McElroy
Peter A. McElroy
Robert E. McEvoy
John A. McFarlane
K. Peter McGarr
Clifford G. McGehee
Patrick J. McGinn
Jack L. McGinnis
Richard W. McGinnis
Walter M. McGriff
James H. McGuire
John D. McHugh
Don J. McIntyre
Marvin C. McKinney
George F. McKnight
W. F. McLendon
T. B. McLeod
Jack McMahan
James C. McMeen
R. W. McMullen
T. D. McNulty
Stan M. McQuain
Leo C. McRoberts
Thomas F. McWhirter
E. D. Meadows
Joseph S. Meadows, D.D.S.
F. E. Meason
Paul L. Meiere, Jr.
Craig Lee Meisel
J. Robert Mell
Frank H. Merl
Dennis Alan Merrick

R. P. Merrill
Clarence Merritt
Paul J. Messer
George S. Miles, Jr.
Alan K. Miller
Charles M. Miller
Clinton A. Miller
Gilbert M. Miller
Jeff B. Miller
James B. Miller Jr.
Joseph Arthur Miller
Joseph N. Miller III
Thomas N. Miller
W. H. Miller
William G. Miller
David P. Mills
J. M. Mills
L. B. Mingledorff
John J. Mion
George Mitchell, D.D.S.
John I. Mitchell
Thomas A. Mitchell
Jan L. Mize
John H. Mobley II
Festus Moncrief
N. Forrest Montet
J. Leo Montgomery
Monty Montrose
Calvin B. Moore
Ernest N. Moore
Henry R. Moore
Howard O. Moore, Jr.
William C. Moore
C. E. Morgan, Jr.
J. L. Morris
John T. Morris
Larry C. Morris
Robert B. Morris
T. Hugh Morris
Thomas F. Morris
Tom A. Morris, Jr.
Tom A. Morris III
John K. Morrow
Michael J. Morse
Phillip D. Mosher
J. B. Mosley
Donald S. Moss
Raymond R. Moss
Stephen J. Motiska
Hon. C. A. Moye, Jr.
Charles A. Muench, Jr.
John M. Muench
Richard A. Meunow
Douglas G. Muir, Jr.
Leon H. Mullins, Jr.
James H. Murphey
Charles N. Murphy, DVM
Michael C. Murphy
Leonard J. Murrans
Robert L. Myatt, Jr.
John A. Myers
Clyde H. Mynatt, Jr.
Dewey T. Nabors, Jr.
Gerald G. Naddra
John F. Nance, Jr.
Charles B. Neal, Jr.
F. Warren Neel
James F. Nellis, Jr.
C. F. Nelson, Jr.
Morris R. Nelson, Jr.
Thomas B. Nelson
Lloyd D. Netherton
Preston E. Newman
W. Joel Newsom, Jr.
Herb J. Newton
Allan D. Nichols
Frank D. Nichols, Jr.
J. Donald Nichols
G. R. Nicholson, Jr.
M. Hugh Nicholson
Roy E. Nimtz
John R. Nisbet, N.D.
Walter E. Nix
James M. Norris, Jr.
Fred A. Nort
Thomas A. Nunnelly
William F. Nygaard

William L. O'Callaghan
Lawrence O'Connor, Jr.
John W. O'Donnell
Milo T. Oakland
Joseph A. Orehosky
Buddy R. Osborne
Garry S. Osley
Charles W. Osterman
Charles T. Otwell
Samuel W. Owen
J. Wayne Owens
Thomas Owings III
James W. Oxendine
William T. Oxford
C. S. Ozburn
Peter E. Paddrik
R. Hoyt Padgett
William D. Padgett
Capers Palmer, Jr., M.D.
Donald F. Palmieri
D. T. Papageorge
Charles M. Parker
James F. Parker
John W. Parker, Jr.
Calvin M. Parsons, Jr.
Norman W. Paschall
Milton E. Pate
Kevin L. Patrick
David F. Patterson
James R. Patterson
William J. Patterson
A. E. Patton
J. L. Patton
Carey B. Paul, Sr.
Carey Brim Paul, Jr.
William T. Paul, Sr.
James Yates Paulding
E. Alan Paulk, Jr., M.D.
George Pavloff
Morgan Q. Payne
R. A. Payne, D.O.
Charles W. Peace, Jr.
Edwin M. Pearce, Jr.
William S. Pearman
C. A. Pearson
Larry Woodrow Pearson
Clarence L. Peeler, Jr.
Eugene Pender
G. W. Pendery
Deric B. Pepler
Thomas F. Perkins
Ben F. Perry, IV
Donald G. Perry, Jr.
Harold R. Perry
Michael J. Perry
Richard C. Perry
George W. Peters
James A. Pettit
H. Wayne Phears
Joseph P. Phelan, Jr.
F. H. Phillips, D.D.S.
James L. Phillips
Logan R. Phillips
Donald L. Phipps
Will H. Pickett
Roscoe Pickett
Larry B. Pickford, M.D.
Robert N. Pickron, D.D.S.
John C. Piede
James H. Pierce
Morris B. Pierce
William G. Pierce
G. Olin Pifer
C. Edward Pike
J. Howard Pike
William L. Pippin
Frederick Pistilli
Charles C. Pittard, Jr.
Louis A. Pittman
Michael S. Pitts
Harold C. Pitts, Jr.
Rex T. Pless
John J. Poole
William F. Pope
Charles R. Porter
William Albright Porter
Don E. Potter

Nick E. Poulos
Malcolm E. Powell
Robert S. Prather, Jr.
John W. Prator
Arlen Ray Price
Harold P. Price
Roy H. Price, Jr.
Edwin P. Pritchett
R. J. Prothro
William L. Pruitt
Charles F. Ptacek
James E. Pudvin
J. Neal Purcell
C. Milburn Purdy
Robert A. Purser, Sr.
Harry H. Purvis
Timothy P. Radigan
Thomas E. Raines
Richard A. Ramsey
James H. Rasnake, Jr.
Harry C. Rawiszer
Larry M. Ray
William I. Ray, Jr.
J. E. Reardon
George A. Reasor
John F. Reaves
Leland H. Reavis
Carroll A. Reddic III
Lester L. Redfern
William B. Redmond, Jr.
Lewis E. Reeves, Jr.
William W. Reichert, M.D.
R. W. Reid, DMD
Charles E. Reiley
Arthur C. Reimann
Richard D. Restagno
Michael P. Reusing
Robert R. Rhinehart
Philip A. Rhodes
Guy H. Richards
W. Frank Richards
Gene Richardson
James G. Richardson
Sam B. Riddick
C. R. Rigdon, D.V.M.
John F. Rilling, Jr.
George A. Rittelmeyer
C. H. Roberts
Frank B. Roberts
Thomas E. Roberts
Thomas Robertson
James J. Robinette
William A. Robinette
Forrest W. Robinson
L. C. Robinson
Marvin L. Robinson
M. M. Robinson
N. W. Robinson
Donald R. Roch
William P. Rocker
David R. Rogers
Henry T. Rogers, Sr.
Joe W. Rogers
Joe W. Rogers, Jr.
Stephen Harry Rogers
Jerry F. Romano
Stephen H. Rosenberg
Albert J. Rosenblatt
Larry T. Ross
Otis R. Rosser
G. S. Rounds, D.C.
Robert W. Rounsaville
John R. Rountree, Jr.
Charles E. Rowland, Jr.
Robert R. Rowland
James A. Royal
Marcus A. Royal
John M. Royall, Jr.
Ford D. Rucker
James M. Rudder
P. R. Rudder
John S. Russell
Edward J. Rutkowski
Allan R. Sackerman
P. E. Sadler
M. Oliver Saggus
John Paul Salb, M.D.

W. T. Sale, M.D.
George H. Salesky
Charles E. Samford
Michael L. Samford
Richard R. Sample
John E. Sampson
Edward S. Sams
H. W. Sams
Hansford Sams, Jr.
Robert B. Sams
Clifton R. Sandford
Don W. Sands
George W. Sands
Steve J. Sands
Raymond H. Sapp
Carl A. Satterlee
Francis B. Saunders
Walter J. Sawicki
G. B. Sawyer
Gerald B. Sawyer
Gerald B. Sawyer, Jr.
Robert Nelson Saxe
Peter Francis Sayeski
W. S. Shackelford
Paul F. Schad
Robert D. Schiller
Marcus H. Schmidt
John S. Schneider
William C. Schuh
F. William Scott
F. R. (Mike) Scudder
Charles W. Seal
Albert Roe Seaman
H. Nathan Sears
Charles E. Seaton
William J. Seay
Ray G. Sechler, Jr.
Dudley R. Segars, Jr.
Edward M. Segars
Gene F. Selawski
Paul H. Senkbeil
Robert E. Senkbeil
Thomas D. Senkbeil
William J. Serravezza
Nelson Severinghaus
Henry L. Sewell, Jr.
Joe M. Sewell
Burton Shackelford
Roger L. Shadburn, Sr.
W. N. Shadburn
H. R. Shadle
Monte Ray Sharp
Yancey L. Shaver
Henry F. Shea, Jr.
Douglas N. Sheley
George W. Shell
William M. Sherwood
Robert P. Shlora
William R. Short
William H. Sibley
Harry P. Siebold, Jr.
Harry P. Siebold, Sr.
Robert G. Siebold
Robert W. Sigle
Bruce W. Simmons
Eddie C. Simmons
Patrick C. Simpson
Morris C. Sims
Hugh Sinclair
Robert P. Sinclair
J. Don Sircy
Howard H. Sisson
F. R. Skipwith
Clifton S. Skow
Jack W. Slaton, Jr.
Joseph J. Slattery, Jr.
Donald W. Sledge
Clifford F. Smiley
Bernard R. Smith
C. W. Smith, M.D.
Charles E. Smith
Charles H. Smith
E. G. Smith, Jr., M.D.
George F. Smith, Jr.
Grant Smith
Guy R. Smith
Ira A. Smith, Jr.

J. W. Smith
Jay B. Smith, III
Joseph L. Smith
Kenneth W. Smith
Oliver M. Smith
Paul W. Smith
Ralph B. Smith
Robert L. Smith
Sheldon E. Smith
Steven D. Smith
T. Donnell Smith
Thomas C. Smith
W. Clay Smith
H. Donald Snapp
Charles V. Snavely
Charles M. Snelling, III
Edward O. Snow
Charles Sockwell, Jr.
Earl S. Soper
Robert R. Sowers
Leon B. Spears, Jr.
Lawson Spence
Edward J. Sperr
John F. Spickerman
W. A. Spitler
Hugh S. Spruill
James E. Stanford
Glenn B. Stangland
Charles M. Stankey
John M. Stanley
James S. Stansberry
Tommy V. Stansell
Paul Stanton, Jr. M.D.
Michael D. Stargel, M.D.
William B. Stark
William B. Stark, Jr.
R. T. Starnes, Jr.
Ray Starnes
Jerry A. Steding
Robert D. Stein
Charles P. Stephens
Howard F. Stephens
John D. Stephens
Wilford C. Stevens, Jr.
Alan G. Stewart
Donald B. Stewart
J. Ed Stewart
James A. Stewart
Terry A. Stewart
Victor M. Stidham
A. J. Stone, M.D.
John C. Stone, Jr.
Samuel A. Stone, Jr.
Thomas E. Story, III
F. J. (Jack) Stow, Jr.
Terry A. Stratton
C. L. Straughan
Charles Lea Strickland
Neil H. Strickland
William J. Strickland
Robert H. Stringer
Robert H. Stringer, Jr.
William S. Stripling
B. J. (Bo) Strong
William F. Stuart, Jr.
William L. Stubbs, Jr.
Gregory E. Stuhler
Berthold G. Stumberg
Brian J. Sturman
J. Everett Summerlin
Jack E. Summers
Kent W. Summers
Moody C. Summers
J. S. Sutherland

James E. Sutherland
Michael H. Sutton
Calvin A. Swaffer
James C. Swaim
James P. Swann, Jr.
David W. Swanson
Dean C. Swanson
R. W. Sweat, D.C.
William S. Swicegood
Jim C. Swink
Louis E. Sylvester
Clyde A. Tallon, Jr.
Ronald R. Tallon
Rene A. Tapia, M.D.
Phillip M. Tatem
Calvin P. Tatum
George A. Taylor
James C. Taylor
Larry E. Taylor, Jr.
Ray N. Taylor
Richard J. Taylor
William J. Teague, Jr.
James Fields Teate
J. L. Tedder
Vincent L. Tedhams
Frank C. Terrell
James H. Terry
Frank R. Tetterton
Donald R. Thacker, Sr.
Mickey F. Thaxton
Robert G. Thesing
William Thigpen
Earl J. Thomas
Patrick M. Thomas
Walter J. Thomas
Dallas S. Thompson
Dewitte Thompson
E. L. Thompson
T. J. (Tommy) Thompson
Y. H. Thompson, Jr.
James A. Thorne
William C. Thornton
J. Everette Thrift
Charles E. Tiller, Jr.
Warren E. Tiller
Paul H. Timmers
Joseph D. Tindall, Jr.
Rufus L. Tindol, Jr.
Rufus L. Tindol III
Stephen C. Tobias
Harold B. Todd, Jr.
Jerry C. Tootle, M.D.
W. Jeffrey Torrence
John K. Totten
Maurice J. Towery
Marvin E. Towner
Charles S. Travis
William F. Trawick
James P. Trimble
David W. True
Harry L. Truitt
C. J. Tucker, Jr.
John W. Tucker
Richard Lee Tucker
Robert P. Tucker, M.D.
K. F. Tulisalo
Barry W. Turk
Robert C. Turk
A. Ronald Turner
D. Glenn Turner
James M. Turner, Jr.
John R. Turner, III
Kyle H. Turner

Larry Turner
Jacob T. Tutterow
John W. Ulfers
John L. Underwood, Jr.
John L. Underwood III
John B. Uttenhove
T. Cole Van Houten
Thomas Van Houten
H. John Vance
Edward Vanderslice
W. H. Vaughan
Lanny S. Vaughn
Arthur G. Vedejs
Edward G. Velazquez
Edward H. Verdery
F. Glenn Verrill
Trammell E. Vickery
G. A. Vollhaber
W. Ray Wactor
Robert F. Wade
R. E. Wagner, Ph.D.
R. Lamar Wakefield
Melvin A. Walbaum
B. Pierce Walker
James C. Walker
L. Roscoe Walker
W. Alford Wall
W. Buice Wallace
Thomas H. Waller
E. Charles Walton
S. Lowell Wammock
James R. Wampler
Warren Ware
Cy E. Warren
J. C. (Jimmy) Warren
M. M. Warren
Terry L. Warren
H. E. Waterhouse
Richard H. Waters
Vincent F. Waters
James C. Watkins
Carl Watson
A. C. Watts
Hal L. Watts
Edward Rex Waylen
Kenneth P. Weatherwax
Jesse J. Webb
Alfred Weeks
Walter W. Weil
Joseph A. Weingartner
Douglas H. Weiss
John A. Wells
John W. Wells
Leo F. Wells, III
Richard H. Wentworth
Richard C. Wernick
Charles Berry West, Jr.
Donovan G. West, Jr.
Richard Charles West
Wm. Preston West
Robert M. Wester
Lawrence D. Wheeler
Warren O. Wheeler
Thomas W. Wheeler, Jr.
Stephen H. Whisenant
C. Sam White
Charles T. White, Jr.
Glenn Steven White
Lowell W. White, Jr.
R. P. White, M.D.
Williston C. White
Harry C. Whitehead
Richard K. Whitehead

Grover M. Whitley
Clyde D. Whitmore
Frank F. Wicker
Alfred A. Wickliffe
Jerry R. Wickliffe
Philip J. Wickstrom
Bruce E. Widener
John H. Wiedeman
Robert S. Wiggins
Tom Wiggins
David C. Wilbanks
Charles S. Wilder, Jr.
A. Lee Wilhelm
William H. Wilkerson
Ted M. Wilkie, Sr.
John Carl Wilkins
Thomas B. Willard
Dwaine L. Willett
B. J. Williams
Byron Robinson Williams, Jr. M.
Dexter H. Williams
G. Lee Williams
James R. Williams
Joseph R. Williams II
L. Harold Williams
Ottis T. Williams
R. Wendell Williams
Richard A. Williams
T. S. Williams III
Thomas L. Williams
Thomas S. Williams, Jr.
Dan H. Williamson, Jr.
E. Wayne Williamson
Hardy T. Williamson
J. R. Williamson, D.D.S.
John B. Willis
Osgood P. Willis
A. E. Wilson, Jr.
John R. Wilson
Thomas M. Wilson
Gene H. Windham
Karl W. Windhorst
Ernest L. Wingard
J. Alton Wingate
John K. Wingfield
Dale F. Wintlend
Charles B. Withers
Russell E. Woerheide
Karl A. Woltersdorf, Jr.
H. Paul Womack
Garnett O. Wood
William A. Wood, Jr.
Mark W. Woods
William W. Woody
W. Rhett Word
William L. Worley
H. Boyd Wright
Joseph Jerry Wright
Harris B. Wynn, III
Tony Yaksh
L. Wayne Yancey
Victor A. Yarborough
H. Cole Yarbrough
Jack Yarbrough
John W. Yost
Dan Young
James M. Young III
Richard J. Young
Richard M. Young
James L. Zahner
Joseph R. Zatto
John Zimmerman
Robert J. Zucker

Oliver P. Ackerman III
Forrest L. Adair III
J. Davis Adams III
Frank J. Adams, Jr.
Robert C. Adams
King V. Aiken, Jr.
Anthony Craig Allen
Mrs. C. K. Allen
Carey Kenneth Allen
Mrs. Daniel J. Allen
D. Carey Allen, Jr.
Julian Brett Allen
Mrs. M. A. Allen
Mrs. W. H. Allen
William R. Allmond
Luther Alverson
Mrs. Joe H. Anderson
James Mason Andrews
Mrs. Charles Applebee
John K. Arney
Scott E. Artinger
Christopher Alan Atkins
Norman E. Atkins
Thomas F. Austin III
John Colin Ayers, Jr.
Mark Kyle Babcock
Kenneth G. Bacheller
Steven E. Bacon
Preston S. Baer
Jack O. Baggett
Kenneth E. Baggett
Robert Cecil Bailey
James G. Bailey, Jr.
Donald W. Baine
Vincent R. Baine
Andrew J. Baker
James M. Ball
Michael Todd Ballard
Charles P. Ballenger
Christopher J. Barber
Wayne Michael Barber
John Frank Barlow, Jr.
Alan L. Barnes, Jr.
Thomas W. Barnes, Sr.
Mrs. Henry T. Barnette
E. M. Barton
Mrs. Walter C. Bass
Mrs. E. A. Bayliss
Jerry W. Beard
Charles T. Beard
Mrs. C. E. Beem
Mrs. V. S. Beem
Joseph A. C. Beeson, Jr.
James Blake Beeson
W. Graves Bell
Michael Bell
Phillip W. Bell
Richard Bell
Mrs. F. Bellinger
Mrs. T. R. Benning, Sr.
Jeffrey F. Benson
Mrs. Norman S. Berg
Mrs. H. S. Bergen, Jr.
George J. Berry
Mrs. Isom A. Berry
James H. Berry
Mrs. Sam M. Berry
Mrs. Bill B. Biggs
Thomas C. Binion
Michael C. Biondo
John David Bittner
Todd Blackburn
Ty Blackburn
Mrs. Edward Blankenship
Jack M. Blasius
Mrs. Harry Boland
Michael Bonallack
Homer P. Bond
John A. Booth
Mrs. John R. Bottomy
David John Bowen
Mrs. Dewey P. Bowen

Larry E. Bowman
Damon S. Boyette
Robert W. Boylston, Jr.
Rev. Jack R. Bozeman
James L. Bracewell
James B. Braden
Stephen S. Bragg
Wm. O. Branch
Mrs. R. M. Braswell
A. T. Bray
Mrs. Arthur R. Brehm
Mrs. W. R. Brewster, Sr.
David L. Bridges
Robert E. Bridges
Thomas Gary Brock
John A. Brocksmith, Jr.
George H. Brodnax IV
Peter D. Brodnax
Mrs. Byron Brooke
Robert B. Brooks
William E. Brooks
George C. Broome III
Charles M. Brown
Jeffrey R. Brown
John Dickson Brown
Mrs. George R. Brown
Mrs. George N. Brown
Mrs. Jno. Brown
Mrs. Nancy S. Brown
Mrs. T. G. Brown
Scott C. Brown
Walter J. Brumit
John K. Bryan
Curtis H. Bryant
Kenneth W. Bryant
Todd Howell Bryant
Mrs. C. S. Buchannan
Lon M. Buckler II
W. Candler Budd
Mrs. L. F. Bunte
Joseph M. Burkhalter
Joe N. Burnett, Jr.
Dana B. Burns
Harris S. (Bill) Burns, III
David Bryan Burruss
George D. Busbee
Billy David Bush
Thomas W. Cadden
Michael John Caldwell
Mrs. L. D. Cale
Wm. R. Callaway
Mrs. R. A. Calvert
Jack J. Camarda, Jr.
William T. Cantrell
George H. Carley, Jr.
Brent A. Carpenter
Mrs. A. F. Carpenter
Richard W. Carpenter, Jr.
Harry L. Cashin III
Philip A. Cashin
Tony G. Cerniglia
Raymond T. Chatham III
Mrs. Larry L. Cheek
John Philip Cheeley
Robert D. Cheeley
Mrs. L. J. Cheely
Mrs. Edgar Cherry
Matthew Allen Childs
Todd Michael Chorba
Mrs. Jack A. Clardy
Danny R. Clark
Matthew J. Clarke
E. M. Clary
William C. Clary, Jr.
Mrs. Roby W. Clay
Roby Clay, Jr.
Mrs. W. L. Clifton, Jr.
Mrs. T. E. Clyatt
Melvin B. Coalson
Gregory M. Coan
Mrs. Charlie K. Cobb
Mrs. J. T. Cobb

Paul D. Cobb
Mrs. L. W. Conger
Mrs. James O. Conley
Mrs. C. T. Conyers
Samuel Kyle Cooley
James H. Cooley, III
David Watson Copeland
Robert Alan Copeland
James E. Copeland III
William G. Cornell, Jr.
Donald Cote
Marc P. Cote
Michael R. Cote
Paul N. Cote
Mrs. W. C. Cottongim
Dean A. Cowart
Daniel Bryan Cowart
Benjamin M. Cowart II
Alec R. Crabbe
David Crawford
William Crawford
William Crawford III
Mrs. James A. Creech
Mrs. C. B. Crenshaw
John E. Crick
Howland E. Crosswell
Mark Crosswell
Russell Allen Crump
Richard H. Culberson, Jr.
David G. Curry
Chris W. Curry
John Scott Curry
John P. Curtis
Kevin R. Curtis
L. H. (Danny) Daniel, Jr.
Mrs. C. L. Davidson, Sr.
Reid H. Davidson
Robert M. Davidson
Clifford A. Davis, Jr.
Douglas A. Davis
Eric S. Davis
Hank Davis
James H. Davis
Mrs. La Vada Davis
Donald W. Dawson
Frank R. Day, O.D.
Martin Peter DeLuca
Gary H. Dean, Jr.
Geoff Smith Dean
Frank M. Deaver III
Mrs. Addison C. Deavours
Mrs. A. M. Deiters
Thomas M. DeLay
James R. Dempsey
Mrs. J. R. Dendinger
Mrs. Donald Devine
Lewis S. Dewberry
Mrs. H. K. Dewees
Jack D. Deweese, Jr.
Peyton Todd Deweese
David Keaton Dick
George P. Dillard
Mrs. John B. F. Dillon, Jr.
John B. F. Dillon III
Mrs. Harry F. Dobbs
Richard G. Donnelly
Thomas P. Donnelly
Mrs. Harold Donohue
David W. Dorman
Daniel J. Dorner
Sean S. Doughtie
Mrs. Floyd K. Dudley
Mrs. G. T. Duke, Sr.
Robert Y. Duke, Jr.
Mrs. Marjorie Durden
Clifton E. Dycus
Charles M. Dykes, Jr.
Derek H. Dykes
Robert W. Eaves III
Mrs. C. M. Eberhart
James R. Echols, Jr.
James L. Eckman

Mrs. Frank E. Edwards
Thoben F. Elrod
Timothy J. Embry
John David Engel, Jr.
Mrs. F. G. Etheridge
Michael S. Evans
Mrs. F. C. Everett, Jr.
Mrs. R. H. Farrar
Carlton L. Ferguson
Norman L. Ferrell, Jr.
Mrs. L. L. Ferry
William E. Fike II
James H. Finch
S. L. (Lan) Finch
Robert Fincher, Jr.
Benjamin Findley
Henry Findley
Joseph C. Finley, Jr.
Christopher A. Fisher
Douglas John Fix
Mrs. W. F. Flaherty
Mrs. M. W. Fletcher
Frank Fling
James K. Flood
P. M. Flood, Jr.
Bryan Patrick Ford
James Andrew Ford
Mrs. George Ford
William W. Forehand
Thomas F. Forkner, Jr.
Thomas B. Fowler III
Mrs. Robert Fowler, Jr.
Major F. Fowler, M.D.
John C. Fredrichs
Lee Samuel Freeman
William N. Freeman
Albert H. Fregosi, Jr.
Gregory K. Gaddis
Cleveland M. Gaddis
Burcher N. Gammage
John G. Gammage, Jr.
A. F. Gandy
R. Gentry Ganote III
Michael P. Ganote
Gary P. Gardner
George C. Gardner
Mrs. James C. Garner
Ms. Mary L. Garretson
Mrs. R. W. Gaston
Mrs. S. B. Gaston
Scott L. Geib
Jeffrey B. Gibbs
Mrs. Arthur Gibson
Brian E. Gilbert
Randall L. Gilbert
Richard S. Gilbert
Curtis Hudson Gill
Jim L. Gillis, Jr.
Charles W. Glass, Jr.
Mrs. Wadley R. Glenn
G. Milton Goolsby
Leonard Gordon III
Mrs. William M. Gordon
Mrs. W. F. Gordy, Jr.
Matthew Forde Gottlich
Anthony J. Governale
Deric Governale
J. A. Gramling
Mrs. Clarence K. Grant
Mrs. George Grant
C. Bruce Grant, Jr.
Daniel Graveline
Doug R. Green
Wm. E. Green III, M.D.
Richard W. Green
W. T. Green, Sr.
Mark T. Greene
W. B. Greene, Jr.
Mrs. W. C. Greenway
Mrs. J. E. Gregory
Mrs. P. E. Gregory
John E. Griffin

Carl C. Grotnes
Mrs. Frank Guess
Steven H. Haase
Michael A. Hale
Michael Scott Hale
William L. Hale, Jr.
Herbert P. Hales
B. Todd Hall
Harold H. Hall
J. Harvey Hall, Jr.
Timothy M. Halstead
James M. Hamilton
William J. Hamilton IV
Mrs. William P. Hammond
Allen A. Hanahan
Philip N. Hanson
Mrs. A. S. Happoldt
William Hardcastle, Jr.
Mrs. W. B. Hare
Joe Frank Harris
Mrs. J. C. Harris, Jr.
Charles M. Harrison
Scott N. Harrison
William Henry Harrison
Daniel Carl Hart
William Wade Hatcher
James W. Heard
H. C. Hearn, Jr.
Robert R. Hearn
Charles B. Hefner, Jr.
Charles H. Heinz
Roy K. Hendee III
James Neal Hendee
E. H. Henderson
Mrs. R. L. Henderson
Russell G. Henderson, Jr.
Daniel E. Henning
Kurt M. Henning
Eric H. Henry
James B. Herndon, Jr.
William F. Herren
C. B. Hewitt, Jr.
Mark S. Heys
Edward S. Heys, Jr.
Robert C. Heyward
William L. Heyward, M.D.
Mrs. R. L. Hickey
James H. Hickman
Glenn Hicks III
John W. Hicks
Curtis O. Hicks, Jr.
Daniel G. Highland
Robert E. Hilburn, Jr.
John A. Hill
Robert J. Hill
Andrew J. Hill, Jr.
Charles L. Hill, Jr.
Eugene August Hill, Jr.
Noel H. Hobgood, Jr.
Robert F. Hochman, Jr.
Scott A. Hoffman
Robert S. Holben
Mrs. Lowery Holden
Kent R. Holding
W. E. Honey
Mark Charles Hood
William B. Hood, II
Mrs. Frank A. Hooper, Jr.
Carl Hayes Hoover
Duane L. Hoover, Jr.
Mrs. Price Horton
Shane R. Houston
George T. Hovis
Bradley James Howard
Mrs. D. T. Howard
Mrs. W. L. Howard
Zachary L. Hubbert
Jim Huber
Charles Hucke
Dallas Scott Hudgens
Jon E. Hudson
William T. Hudson, III
Mrs. Claude Huey
Claude L. Huey, III
Thomas M. Huff
C. E. Hughes
David Scott Hughes

Mel L. Hughes
Mrs. Lester Hughes, Jr.
Robert W. Hughes, Jr.
Rufus T. Hulsey
John C. Humphries
C. Lawrence Hunsaker
Kevin T. Hunter
R. Daran Hunter
Charlton A. Huntley
Howell V. Hurston
John M. Hyatt
Kenneth C. Hyde
Billy Hyde
David C. Hydrick
R. Beverly Irwin
Russell Ivie
Barry Keith Jackson
Brad K. Jackson
David Willis Jackson
Michael H. Jackson
Mrs. L. H. Jackson
Michael Ray Jamison
Mrs. W. W. Jefferson
Ben H. Jenkins, M.D.
Mrs. Bruce E. Jennings
Mrs. Roger H. Jennings
Bruce E. Jennings, III
Keith Alan Jernigan
Charles A. Jerol
Randall John Jewell
Brad Johns
Scott B. Johnson
Charles M. Johnson
E. Paul Johnson
Mrs. Guy Johnson
Mrs. Martin L. Johnson
Mrs. Trawick Johnson
Russell P. Johnson
Tommy Johnson
Clayton Robert Jones
Leah Paulette Jones
Mary Helen Jones
Gregory Allen Jones
Robert T. Jones IV
Mrs. Charles R. Jones
Mrs. H. H. Jones
Mrs. R. A. Jones
Mrs. Robert M. Jones
Mrs. Roy L. Jones
Robert P. Jones, III
Edmund W. Jones, Jr.
Maj. H. H. Jordan
Mrs. William M. Jordan
Robert J. Jordan
Michael E. Justice
Dana W. Karschner
Mrs. Lee A. Kays
J. N. Keelin
James F. Keith
Richard E. Kelly
James P. Kelly III
Edward J. Kennedy, Jr.
F. F. Kennedy, Jr.
Brant Alan Kenney
James Walter Kiker
Galen B. Kilburn
Anthony M. Kindred
Judy King
Dorothy Kirby
James L. Kirk, II
Mrs. Paul S. Kirkland
Thomas W. Kiser
Gordon P. Kiser, III
Joel J. Knight
W. Clark Knippers
Bradford C. Koontz
Mrs. A. J. Kroog
Brad M. Kuehn
Eric F. Kuehn
Jeffery Alan Kuehn
Joe T. LaBoon, Jr.
Thad Howard Lane
R. Christopher Lane
E. R. Langley
Mrs. G. M. Lawrence
Mrs. John C. Lawton
Kyle C. Leach

Mrs. Wallace L. Lee
Mrs. William Leide
Michael E. Lester
Mrs. Thomas R. Lester
Gary C. Lewis
Sidney A. Lewis
Mrs. Thomas Lide
Mrs. Don A. Limbert
Tsun-hsien Lin
Manfred H. H. Linkogel
Harold L. Lipham
William D. Little
Mrs. R. I. Lively
Mrs. W. W. Lively
Mrs. Frank Lupy
Charles A. Lusted
W. B. Macke
K. R. T. Mackenzie
Robert G. Magbee
Jim E. Magee
Scott T. Mairose
Mrs. Steven A. Manthe
Arch S. Martin
Mrs. Charles S. Martin
David Kevin Martin
Mrs. L. P. Martin
Mrs. Roger A. Martin
Scott C. Martin
Joe R. Martin, Jr.
Patrick L. Mathis, Jr.
Mrs. L. V. Matthews
Ted S. Mauldin, Jr.
Walter Lee Mauney
Donald A. Maxey
Lary V. Maxey
Warren H. May
Mrs. Wade M. Mayo
Hardy McCalman
Michael C. McCloud
Mark W. McCord
James M. McCormick
Robert McCreary, Jr.
C. R. (Roddy" McCrory
Steve McCuiston
Walter P. McCurdy, III
Joes A. McDade
Mrs. H. P. McDonald
Peter L. McDonald
Alonzo L. McDonald, Jr.
Mrs. N. B. McDonough
Michael S. McDowell
Charles W. McDowell, III
Brian F. McEvoy
Kevin Patrick McEvoy
R. Sean McEvoy
C. Graham McGehee, IV
Sam P. McGill
Andrew H. McGinnis
Mrs. Paul J. McGovern
James P. McInnis
Jeffery D. McInnis
Mrs. Wade K. McInnis
W. K. (Rick) McInnis, Jr.
Mrs. T. H. McKey, Jr.
William Alan McKnight
G. S. McKnight
M. Sean McLendon
Mrs. A. E. McLendon
J. K. McLendon, M.D.
C. B. McManus
Robert G. McNair
Mrs. Edward L. McNiff
Homer N. Meier
Paul L. Meiere, III
L. A. Menzel
Andrew Frank Merl
John Clinton Merrick
Paul J. Messer, Jr.
William P. Middlemas
Frank J. Miles
Joseph F. Miller
Kevin Andrew Miller
Mark J. Miller
Stephen C. Miller
Tap C. Miller
Todd M. Miller
Wm. H. Miller, Jr.

Bryan Taylor Mills
Mrs. B. W. Mills, Jr.
Mrs. Richard M. Mills
Mrs. Harris Mills, Sr.
Mrs. C. S. Mingledorff
John J. Mion, Jr.
W. C. Mitchell
Jonathan Lee Mize
L. D. Montague
Johnny L. Montgomery
Phillip F. Moon
Charles Moore
Jason K. Moore
Mrs. William L. Moore
Wiley L. Moore, Jr.
Jesse B. Moreland, Jr. DDS
Clifford E. Morgan III
Mrs. Thomas S. Morgan
J. T. Morgan, Jr.
Mrs. Roy F. Morgan, Sr.
J. R. Morris
Shan Wilder Morris
Mrs. W. K. Moseley
Don D. Mullins
Frank B. Murphy
C. Mark Murphy
D. Jay Murphy
Mrs. Stuart P. Murray
Mrs. Richard F. Muske
Mrs. Hiram Abif Myers
Clyde K. Mynatt
Jeffrey G. Mynatt
Michael G. Naddra
Frank Warren Neel, Jr.
Larry Nelson
Charles T. Nelson, Jr.
Morrie R. Nelson
Andrew J. Netherton
Cass E. Netherton
W. Joel Newsom III, D.D.S.
Mrs. Edward T. Newton
Andrew D. Nichols
Mrs. Frank D. Nichols
Timothy C. Nichols
John R. Nicholson
Robert W. Nicholson
S. A. Nunn, Jr.
Mrs. Eugene W. O'Brien
Diana L. O'Callaghan
John P. O'Callaghan
William C. O'Kelley
William C. O'Kelly, Jr.
Joe F. Oliver
Mrs. Ray R. Olds
Stephen P. Orehosky
Mrs. R. Hoe Osgood
Garry S. Osley, II
Raymond C. Otwell
Mrs. Frank C. Owens
Thomas Owings IV
John W. Oxendine
Michael T. Oxford
Leonard D. Pace, D.M.D.
Mrs. Fred N. Palmer
Mrs. John D. Palmerlee
Thomas H. Paris
James F. Parker, Jr.
Mrs. Ben H. Parks
Mrs. James M. Parks
Jerry K. Pate
Kirby E. Pate
Milton E. Pate, Jr.
Mrs. E. K. Patton
Mrs. Robert B. Paul
Bobby Pavloff
Thomas J. Pavloff
Mr. Roy A. Pearson, Jr.
W. B. Pebworth
Mrs. W. N. Pendleton
Richard H. Pennell
M. K. Pentecost
Mrs. William J. Peterson
William C. Peterson
Steven P. Phipps
Donald L. Phipps, II
Mrs. Frank L. Picotte
Jeffrey M. Piede

Mrs. J. V. Pierotti
Graham Pifer
Charles C. Pittard III
L. Arnie Pittman
Lamar R. Plunkett
H. Mark Plunkett
Michael E. Podolak
Mrs. E. H. Polzin
Mrs. John M. Poole
David F. Pope
Mrs. Bradley T. Porter
Phil T. Porter
Brian E. Powell
Steven Malcolm Powell
Mrs. Bert F. Prather
Mark Alan Price
David P. Price
Robert Priest
Matt Edwin Pritchett
Todd P. Pritchett
Jay E. Pudvin
Robert A. Purser, Jr.
V. O. Rankin, Jr.
Kevin P. Reardon
James E. Reardon, III
Todd A. Reasor
Raymond F. Redden
Carroll A. Reddic IV
Mrs. J. L. Reddick, Jr.
Mrs. A. F. Rees IV
Robert D. Reusing
Mrs. J. O. Rhyne
Clyde G. Rice
Scott Rich
Mrs. F. E. Rich
R. Kirk Rich
Mrs. Charles C. Rife
Charles R. Ridgon, Jr.
Robert W. Ritter
John J. Roberts, Jr.
Michael B. Robinson
Mrs. Con Robinson
Richard W. Robinson
William Blount Robinson
Mrs. William M. Robinson
J. F. (Rick) Romano
Gerald R. Romberg
Mrs. C. A. Rose
Edward J. Royal
Robert Clark Rudder III
Kevin Brian Rudder
Michael E. Turkowski
Mrs. G. W. Rutland, Jr.
William A. Salter
Mrs. Philip K. Sanders
Mrs. Clinton L. Sanders
Harold L. Sargent
J. Douglas Sargent, Jr.
Davis B. Sawyer
Lee B. Schemmel
Mrs. R. W. Schilling
James W. Scott
Mark A. Scudder
Michael R. Scudder
Robert H. Sealey
Brian B. Seay
Joe Sewell, Jr.
Roger L. Shadburn, Jr.

William E. Shadle
James O. Shealy, Jr.
Mrs. I. M. Sheffield
Thomas A. Sherard
Mrs. Robert P. Shinall
Kazuo Shiratori
J. Frank Shoaf
Mrs. Herman Short, Jr.
William J. Shortt
Harold E. Shrader
Mrs. Evans L. Shuff
Mrs. Robert C. Shutts
Scott A. Siebold
Robert W. Sigle, Jr.
Maurice W. Simmons
Michael N. Simmons
James W. Sinclair
Mrs. Paul A. Sinclair
Gerald W. Sircy
Steven D. Sircy
Boyd Sloan
Clifford F. Smiley, Jr.
Scott H. Smith
Cary Benjamin Smith
David A. Smith
James B. Smith
Joey M. Smith
John Clayton Smith
John H. Smith
M. M. Smith
Michael B. Smith
Steven D. Smith
Steven Lee Smith
George F. Smith III
J. S. Smith, Jr.
Bartow R. Snooks
Rev. J. W. Sosebee
Mrs. J. H. Souther
Jeffery G. Spence
John P. Sperr
Charles Edward Sperr
Mrs. A. C. Spinks
George N. Spring
Mrs. M. M. Springer
Marvin M. Springer, Jr.
Eric Scott Stanton
D. Mark Starnes
Albert H. Staton
James M. Steding
Leslie J. Steele, Jr.
Jimmie R. Stein
Roderic G. Steinkamp
Mrs. R. L. Stephens
J. B. Stephens
Mar, W. Stephens
Davis C. Stewart
Gary L. Stewart
J. Scott Stewart
Mrs. George E. Stewart
James A. Stewart, Jr.
Terry A. Stewart, Jr.
Leslie W. Stitt, Jr.
Mrs. Albert W. Stout
Mrs. W. O. Street
Mrs. W. W. Stribling
Clifton H. Strickland
Todd Stripling
Moody C. Summers IV

Jay Driskell Swaim
Anthony L. Swann
Dean Stewart Swanson
Warren R. Sweat
Matthew H. Sweat
William T. Swicegood
M. F. Swilley, Jr., D.C.
Mrs. Clyde V. Swofford
Stan S. Swofford
Douglas H. Sylvester
Mike R. Tapia
Michael A. Tatum
Mrs. Luther S. Tatum
W. P. Tatum, Jr.
Timothy Taylor
C. W. Taylor, Jr.
Richard T. Tedhams
Robert M. Thaxton
Carol Semple Thompson
Christopher F. Thompson
Thomas J. Thompson III
Mrs. R. L. Thompson
David M. Thornton
Charles J. Thurmond
R. Austin Tilghman, Jr.
Robert Tiller
Paul H. Timmers, Jr.
Mrs. J. D. Tindall, III
Charles L. Tindol
Michael L. Tindol
Harold B. Todd III
Jerry C. Tootle, Jr.
Mrs. W. I. Truitt, Jr.
E. Barry Tsitouris
Richard N. Tucker
Robert P. Tucker III
Clyde Cebron Tuggle
Mrs. Arthur Tuggle
Christopher D. Turner
Mrs. H. L. Turner
Mrs. J. E. Turner
T. Paul Turner
W. H. Turner
Joe Bar Turner
Paul L. Turner, Jr.
Samuel T. Tutterow
Jodge E. P. Tuttle
Douglas M. Underwood
Martin N. Underwood
J. L. Underwood, IV
Andrew J. Velazquez
Michael S. Velazquez
Gary G. Verrill
Steven H. Vining
Joe S. Wade
Mrs. B. E. Wagstaff
Mrs. Sharpe Wall
Thomas Craig Waller
Richard P. Wampler
Mrs. Delmar K. Ward
Matthew Lee Warren
Mrs. David G. Warner
Christian M. Warren
Michael E. Warren
Kent J. Wascovich
Rev. G. E. Wascovich
John T. Wasdin
Thomas J. Washburn

Jonathan E. Waterhouse
Harold L. Watson
Hal Watts, Jr.
Kenneth Weatherwax, Jr.
Scott H. Weatherwax
J. Mark Webb
Mrs. John Wesley Weekes
Mrs. Robert B. Wehrman
David W. Weiss
John W. Wells
Leo Fred Wells, IV
Earle B. Welsh, Jr.
James B. Wernick
Rev. James Wesberry
Mrs. Wesley W. West
Steven Glenn West
Mrs. Charles E. Whalen
Charles H. Wheatley
Mrs. W. A. Wheeler
Robert L. Whelan
C. Bartow Whitaker III
Mrs. Charles E. White
Dan White
Lamar B. White
Lamont K. White
Mrs. W. O. White
Norman Lee White
C. Sam White II
Bradley A. Whitehead
Cass Whitehead
Kent E. Whitehead
Mrs. C. H. Whitehead
R. K. Whitehead, III
George P. Whitlock
Dana P. Whitlow
Mrs. Geo. P. Whitman, Jr.
James Ross Whitmore
Philip J. Wickstrom, Jr.
Justin H. Wiedeman
Harold F. Wiedeman
Ben T. Wiggins
Llewellyn Wilburn
Mrs. L. W. Wilcox
David M. Wilder
John B. Williams
Mrs. Ralph W. Williams
Dale G. Williamson
Jason R. Willis
Jeffrey W. Willis
John B. Willis, Jr.
Mrs. John E. Wilsher
Hugh W. Wilson
Robert Cobb Wilson
John A. Woerheide
H. Paul Womack III
Garnett O. Wood
Gary D. Woods
Mrs. William A. Woods
Jack W. Worley
J. R. "Ric" Yarbrough
Kenneth Cole Yarbrough
Charles R. Yates
John R. Yost
Christopher B. Zatto
James R. Ziegelbaur, Jr.
John Mark Zimmerman
Mrs. Leslie F. Zsuffa
Mrs. John W. Zuber

135

NOTES ON THE AUTHOR

Nancy Neill developed a fascination for the folklore and history of the South as a child in her native Mississippi. As an Atlantan for the past decade, she has become known for her articles on local history and personalities, including humorous essays which have appeared in *Business Atlanta* magazine. Her work has also appeared in *Atlanta* magazine, *Atlanta Weekly, Inc.* magazine, and numerous other publications.

Selected as a Fulbright Scholar upon graduation from the University of Mississippi, she spent a year in New Zealand, where she completed a book comparing the fictional treatment of the native American and the native New Zealander. She also holds a master's degree in English literature from the University of California.